Wealth Management

Steven M. Bragg

AccountingTools®

ISBN 978-1-64221-335-5

For more information about AccountingTools® products, visit our Web site at www.accountingtools.com.

Table of Contents

Chapter 1 - Baseline Information for Financial Planning 1

Introduction 1

Life Planning 1

Translating Life Planning into Financial Policies 2

Identify Funding Tranches 3

Identify Timing of Goals 3

Identify Lifestyle Costs 4

Discuss Retirement 4

Consider Your Withdrawal Plans 4

Identify Your Risk Profile 5

Identify Your Investment Management Style 8

Summary 9

Chapter 2 - The Financial Plan 10

Introduction 10

Your Current Financial Position 10

    Liquidity Analysis 10

    Investments in Private Businesses 11

Your Planning Assumptions 11

The Cash Flow Projection 12

Plan Adjustments 13

Your Investment Strategy 13

    Portfolio Rebalancing 13

    Tax-Loss Harvesting 14

    The Use of Leverage 14

    Dollar-Cost Averaging 15

    Sector Rotation 15

Summary 16

Chapter 3 - Financial Advisors 17

Introduction 17

The Need for Steady Advice 17

The Certified Financial Planner 18

The Ideal Advisor 18

Advisory Fees *19*

Advisor Evaluation Questions *20*

Disadvantages of Using a Financial Advisor *21*

Summary *21*

Chapter 4 - Wealth Preservation **22**

Introduction *22*

Investment Principles *22*

Speculation and Investing *23*

Investment Risk *24*
    Fixed Income Risk 24
    Equity Risk 25

The Basic Investment Types *26*
    Ownership Investments 26
        Stock Market Investments 26
        Real Estate Investments 27
        Business Ownership Investments 27
    Lending Arrangements 27
        Savings Instruments 27
        Debt Reduction 28
    Risk and Investing 28
        Mitigating the Risk of a Decline in Market Value 29
        Mitigating the Risk of a Decline in a Specific Investment 30
        Mitigating the Risk of Inflation 30
        FDIC Coverage 30

Summary *31*

Chapter 5 - Investing in Stocks **32**

Introduction *32*

How Businesses Raise Money *32*

How Businesses Add Value *32*

Characteristics of Stocks *34*

The Stock Market *34*

Market Moving Events *35*

Bull Markets and Bear Markets *36*

Investing Strategies *37*
    Mutual Funds 40

A Word on Speculative Bubbles *40*
    Penny Stock Concerns 41

A Word on Money Manager Performance *41*

How to Judge Your Investing Performance *42*

Summary *42*

Chapter 6 - Investing in Lending Arrangements **43**

Introduction *43*

Characteristics of Lending Arrangements *43*

Lending Choices *43*

    Banks 43

    Money Market Funds 44

    Bonds 45

        Types of Bonds 46

        Bond Features 46

        Bond Investment Considerations 47

        The Yield Curve 48

        U.S. Government Debt Instruments 49

        State and Local Government Debt 50

        Corporate Bonds 50

How to Buy Bonds *51*

Summary *52*

Chapter 7 - Investing in Funds **53**

Introduction *53*

Mutual Funds vs. Exchange-Traded Funds *53*

Fund Investment Best Practices *55*

    Reduce Fund Costs 55

    Look for Consistent Returns 57

    Avoid Taxes 57

    Allocate Assets 57

    Avoid Leveraged Funds 57

    Invest in Experience 57

Stock Fund Fundamentals *58*

Bond Fund Fundamentals *59*

Bond Fund Selection Process *60*

Hybrid Funds *61*

Summary *61*

Chapter 8 - Investing in Property **62**

Introduction *62*

Advantages of Investing in Real Estate *62*

Disadvantages of Investing in Real Estate *64*

Types of Real Estate Investments...*66*
    Purchase a Residence 66
    Convert a Residence to a Rental..66
    Upgrade and Sell Your Home 67
    Buy a Second Home 67
    Buy a Timeshare..68
    Buy a Residential Property 69
    Flip a Residential Property 70
    Buy Commercial Property 70
    Buy Undeveloped Land 71

How to Acquire Real Estate..*72*
    Foreclosures...72
    Probate Sales 74
    Short Sales 75

Installment Sales..*76*

Real Estate Investment Trusts...*77*

Real Estate Investment Best Practices *78*

Summary...*80*

Chapter 9 - Investing in Alternative Investments **81**

Introduction..*81*

Call Options *81*

Put Options *81*

Currencies *81*

Hedge Funds...*82*

Venture Capital *83*

Precious Metals *83*

Works of Art..*84*

Collectibles...*84*

Raw Land..*85*

Timberland Investments..*85*

Summary...*86*

Chapter 10 - Individual Retirement Accounts **87**

Introduction *87*

Overview of Individual Retirement Accounts *87*
    Individual Retirement Account (IRA) 87
    Roth IRA 88
    IRA and Roth IRA Comparison 88
    Rollover IRA 90

Savings Incentive Match Plan for Employees (SIMPLE) 91
Simplified Employee Pension (SEP) IRA 91

Ability to Contribute to an IRA 92

Caps on IRA Contributions 93
Contribution Caps for Singles 93
Contribution Caps for Spouses 93
Excess Contributions 94

Deductibility of IRA Contributions 94

Allowable Distributions 96

Early Distribution Penalties 96

Taxability of IRA Interest 97

Required Minimum Distributions 97

Qualified Charitable Distributions 97

Summary 98

Chapter 11 - Socially Responsible Investing 99

Introduction 99

ESG Investing 99

Thematic Investments 100

Summary 101

Chapter 12 - The Role of Insurance in Wealth Management 102

Introduction 102

Property Insurance 102
Types of Property 102
Policy Inclusions 102
Policy Exclusions 103
Additional Coverages 103
Valuation Issues 104
Remedial Activities 104

Life Insurance 105
Varieties of Life Insurance 106

Annuities 107

Summary 108

Chapter 13 - Charitable Contributions 109

Introduction 109

The Nature of a Charitable Contribution 109

Qualified Charitable Organizations 109

Types of Allowable Contributions *109*

Contributions from Which You Benefit *110*

Property Contributions *111*

The Determination of Fair Market Value *114*

Deduction Recapture *117*

Contributions that are Not Deductible *118*

Penalties *119*

Substantiation Requirements *119*
    Substantiation of Cash Contributions 119
    Substantiation of Noncash Contributions 120
    Substantiation of Out-of-Pocket Expenses 120

Summary *121*

Glossary **122**

Index **126**

About the Author

Steven Bragg, CPA, has been the chief financial officer or controller of four companies, as well as a consulting manager at Ernst & Young. He received a master's degree in finance from Bentley College, an MBA from Babson College, and a Bachelor's degree in Economics from the University of Maine. He has been a two-time president of the Colorado Mountain Club, and is an avid alpine skier, mountain biker, and certified master diver. Mr. Bragg resides in Centennial, Colorado. He has written more than 300 books and courses, including *New Controller Guidebook*, *GAAP Guidebook*, and *Payroll Management*. He has also written the science fiction novel *Under an Autumn Sun*, first book in *The Auditors* trilogy.

Steven maintains the accountingtools.com web site, which contains continuing professional education courses, the Accounting Best Practices podcast, and thousands of articles on accounting subjects.

Chapter 1
Baseline Information for
Financial Planning

Introduction

It is essential to adopt a plan for how you go about the process of obtaining and managing wealth. Most people do not follow this maxim; instead, they have only a general idea of what their financial goals may be, and bounce from the advice of one financial guru to the next. To bring clarity to the situation, it is essential to first understand the nature of your life goals, such as being a champion polo rider (expensive) or a monk (less expensive). With that information in hand, you can then step down a notch to determine your financial goals. Maintaining a string of polo ponies will require some robust wealth management, while it is less of an issue if you plan to meditate in a cave.

In this book, we cover a wide range of issues pertaining to wealth management, including life planning, your financial plan, wealth preservation, investment options, insurance, charitable contributions, and much more.

Life Planning

As noted in the introduction, the first step in wealth management is ascertaining your life goals, since they define how much money you will need. The most common issue in this area is that people do not attempt to set any life goals, and so bounce through life, grasping at opportunities that have no relation to their preferences, while too easily abandoning activities that might make them happier in the long run. The result is financial planning that has no basis in an underlying life structure, and which results in far too little wealth (the usual state of affairs) or more wealth than a person can possibly handle.

The reverse situation can also arise, where people (frequently entrepreneurs) throw themselves into a business, eventually sell out for a substantial sum – and then lose all reason to get up in the morning, because they have never set any life goals that extended beyond the workplace.

There is no perfect life plan – it is unique to each individual. Consequently, you should spend a significant amount of time thinking about what is most important to you (such as living in the mountains or on a beach, or being a full-time artist), as opposed to doing things that you are obliged to do (such as child and parent care). Truly important items tend to cover many years, and can be differentiated from short-term "bucket list" items, such as visiting Prague, or participating in the running of the bulls in Pamplona. Another way to discern important items is to think about where you would like to spend a significant amount of your wealth – in effect, putting your money where your heart is. Out of this analysis might come a determination that you *really* want to live in Hawaii, or support a child's desire to be a professional ski racer, or write the Great American Novel. It also might lead you to conclude that some "wish list" items are not that important, such as climbing the highest point in every county in the country, of which there are 3,142 (that is an actual goal for several people).

Your life planning analysis might include a focus on specific activities, in which you are willing to invest a significant amount of time. Here are some of the more common activity goals that people consider to be important:

- Attain a specific position (perhaps as the leader of a nonprofit, or a certain management job)
- Be a successful artist (perhaps defined as writing a book, selling a painting, or performing music)
- Be a successful parent (perhaps defined as attending all school events, or assisting with learning)
- Be financially successful (perhaps defined as annual income or net worth)
- Be physically fit (which can be refined down into specific sports)
- Be politically active (perhaps with a certain position as a goal, such as being a representative at the state level)
- Be well educated (for which you can identify a specific level of schooling, such as a master's degree)
- Be well traveled (this is a great place to employ a bucket list, for places to visit)
- Learn a new skill (such as locksmithing, carpentry, rock climbing, etc.)
- Learn another language (with some definition of the level of learning attained; this may include living in another country for a period of time)

One life goal that is of particular concern is the concept of being physically fit. Doing so may prolong your lifespan, which in turn impacts the amount of money you will need for the rest of your life. Consequently, it can be useful to research how a population's average lifespan is impacted by certain types of physical activity. For example, endurance training tends to yield the longest lifespan, while power training yields more modest results.

The key items in a life plan are those that are non-negotiable. You feel that you absolutely must do them – such as visiting every Gothic cathedral in France, or attending the Monterey Jazz Festival, or producing a documentary on the breeding habits of the two-toed sloth. Funding will likely be required for these key items, so paying for them will be part of your financial planning activities.

Translating Life Planning into Financial Policies

Once you have a general idea of your life planning goals, you can use them as the basis for a set of financial policies. These policies are intended to be guiding principles that structure how you make financial decisions. Financial policies should be sufficiently detailed that they provide guidance for most of the financial situations you are likely to encounter. For example, you could set up the following policies to provide structure to your wealth management activities:

- I will only invest in the shares of companies within the S&P 500 stock index that pay dividends.
- I will always maintain a minimum of $100,000 in a money market account.
- I will maintain enough life insurance to pay for the remaining educational expenses of my children, through graduate school.
- I will not invest in the business ventures of other family members.
- I will give 5% of my gross income to qualified nonprofit entities.
- I will reject all offers to work overtime.
- I will not work on activities that breach my ethical commitments.

One way to set up financial policies is to review the questions you periodically face when spending or investing cash, and decide which policies would have given you structure in those cases. For example, if a brother-in-law persistently asks you for money to support his lawn care business, you can set up a policy to not invest in any family ventures.

Identify Funding Tranches

When devising a financial plan, it can be useful to break your financial requirements into three categories. The first and most important is the funding needed to support the key items in your life plan – those that are non-negotiable. There may be a cheaper way to support these items, but their funding must, at all costs, be included in the plan. The second category is for desired items, such as gifting money to a favored niece, or buying a sports car, or owning a vacation home. These items are not as critical, so the funding for them is not as important. Finally, there are ambitious goals, which you only expect to pursue if there is sufficient funding for all other goals. For example, you might aspire to increase your contributions to a treasured charity, or perhaps fund a scholarship for needy students.

Identify Timing of Goals

As part of the planning process, settle upon the dates by which cash requirements will arise. For example, you might want to buy a vacation home in two years, or fund a daughter's wedding in one year, or sail around the world in your own sailboat in ten years. These dates will have a significant impact on your financial planning. For example, a need to pay for a vacation home in two years presents the need to avoid capital losses in the short term, which can drive changes to your investment strategy. Conversely, if you want to sail around the world in ten years, then short-term capital losses are less of a concern; instead, you might be more concerned about how inflation could cut into your savings over the intervening ten years – which will impact the nature of your investments.

Identify Lifestyle Costs

A key ingredient of any financial plan is a solid estimate of your projected lifestyle costs. These costs should be based on a combination of your current spending and what you plan to spend in the future while pursuing your life goals. Many people have only the vaguest idea of how much they spend now. Tracking your current expenditures on an electronic spreadsheet is an excellent way to gain a better understanding of your spending. A further consideration is that many people have a hard time scaling back on their current expenditures, making it difficult to adhere to a future in which you are spending less money. For example, if you currently spend $2,000 a year on a theatre ticket subscription, you might not want to give it up after you retire – which can throw your financial plans into disarray. In addition, do not assume that "one-time" expenditures will only arise once; generally, one-time expenditures keep occurring – just at fairly long intervals. Therefore, these items will need to be accounted for within a financial plan.

It is quite likely that you will not initially do a good job of identifying ongoing lifestyle costs. That is quite all right; just keep reviewing them year after year, and you will eventually find that most categories of expenditures tend to recur in approximately the same amounts, on an ongoing basis. In short, once you have an expenditure history, you can more easily project costs into the future.

Discuss Retirement

Are you really planning to retire at 65? Many people are interested in working longer, perhaps in a reduced role, or in a different job entirely. Others are so wrapped up in their work that they have no interest in ever stopping, and so continue working for several decades past the normal retirement age. Conversely, some people have a deep interest in scaling back before they reach retirement age, perhaps to make retirement less of a shock when they eventually reach retirement age and leave the workforce entirely. In short, due consideration of these issues could result in a significantly different financial plan, since it has a major impact on the amount and duration of your income.

Consider Your Withdrawal Plans

It may be necessary to periodically withdraw funds from your investments. These withdrawals may be needed to fund your lifestyle, or to make specific purchases (such as a car replacement). This is an accepted part of wealth management for many people, since their ongoing income receipts will typically decline drastically following their retirement. The amount of this periodic withdrawal should be carefully modeled, since you may run out of money if the withdrawals exceed a certain amount or are made too frequently. Also, if your securities holdings are risky and therefore produce volatile results, ongoing withdrawals can result in a rapid drop in your fund balance. This latter outcome arises when you continue to withdraw funds even during periods when volatility has produced substantial negative returns, resulting in a rapid decline in your investment balance.

There are several methods available for withdrawing funds, including the following:

- Take the interest and dividends produced by your portfolio, rather than reinvesting it. This approach requires little monitoring, since the underlying investments are not touched.
- Withdraw a fixed amount per year, no matter what the return from your investments may be. This approach requires more monitoring, to ensure that you do not drive your investment balance down too low. This can be a particular problem during the early years, when an adverse change in your portfolio's value, coupled with withdrawals, could result in a substantially reduced portfolio in later years.
- Withdraw a percentage of the portfolio each year. This will result in a varying withdrawal amount, as the value of the underlying portfolio changes. If you have risky investments with volatile returns, this will result in significant changes in the amounts withdrawn. Conversely, safer investments will result in more consistent withdrawals from year to year.

> **Tip:** Model your withdrawal plan using lower rates of return or lower levels of annual withdrawals, to see how this impacts the viability of your plan.

There is no perfect withdrawal method – it all depends on how much cash you need, the variability of the returns from your investments, and how much cash you want to retain in your investments.

> **Tip:** When deciding upon a withdrawal strategy, you could use the *four percent rule*, which states that retirees can safely withdraw an amount equal to four percent of their savings in each year. This is only a general guideline, but can form the basis for more detailed withdrawal planning that takes into account your needs, the volatility of returns from your investment, tax rates, and so forth. Of course, if you can afford to withdraw a smaller percentage, this reduces the risk that you will exhaust the funds in your portfolio. If you are invested primarily in fixed-income securities, then your returns will be lower, so your withdrawal percentage will likely need to be less than the four percent rule.

Identify Your Risk Profile

A key part of wealth management is ascertaining the level of financial risk that you can comfortably support. The generation of high rates of return on investments usually requires that you also take on a higher risk of loss, since higher returns are generally associated with a higher level of risk. For example, you might have to support a series of losses on a risky investment that reacts adversely to declines in economic conditions, in order to reap higher returns during periods when the economy is more robust. This can result in protracted periods of losses – so, can you sleep well at night, knowing that you might sustain losses for several years? If so, then there are a variety of higher-risk investments that you might consider acquiring. Conversely, if you prefer a nice, steady return, then that can also be arranged, but your returns from these investments will be lower than if you could support a higher risk profile. In short, your risk profile will dictate the types of investments that you purchase.

As an example of how the risk-return issue can impact your wealth management, you want to fly aerobatic airplanes during your retirement years, but the $600,000 cost of the necessary plane and ongoing operating fees make this goal impossible, unless you are willing to earn more money, spend less money, or invest in riskier investments during the years leading up to your retirement. If the first two options are not possible, then your sole remaining choice is riskier investments. Deciding to take this third option will likely require some consideration of whether the aerobatics goal is sufficiently important to make you willing to incur some sleepless nights thinking about potential investment losses.

As another example, you are a state-level government bureaucrat who is assured of receiving a solid pension through your retirement years. Given the security of this income, you might be willing to undertake a higher degree of risk in your investments, knowing that you are backstopped by a solid source of ongoing pension income. As yet another example, you are a successful entrepreneur who earns a substantial income from your business. In this case, your ongoing cash flows are so positive that you are more inclined to take risks on your investments, since any capital losses can be easily replenished. In short, your risk profile will depend to some extent on your financial circumstances.

There may be cases in which your financial circumstances are quite solid, with lots of assured income – and yet you are emotionally uncomfortable with the prospect of losing money on your investments. This represents a low level of risk tolerance, which is based on a combination of your personality traits, upbringing, life experiences, and education. This situation is entirely normal; do not try to stretch your risk tolerance to the point where certain types of investments are making you uncomfortable.

Tip: You may be able to compartmentalize a low level of risk tolerance by setting aside portions of your investments for different purposes. For example, a reserve fund for rainy days might be parked in a no-risk money market account, while an education fund for your child's college tuition is associated with a slightly higher-risk blue chip stock index, and a small long-term investment fund is targeted at riskier investments. By only setting aside a modest amount for high-risk investments, you might be able to control your risk-averse nature.

Your risk profile can change over time, based on your experiences. For example, during a lengthy bull run in the stock market, it might appear that stock prices go nowhere but up, so you grow increasingly comfortable pouring the bulk of your savings into stock investments – which is reasonable, based on your near-term experience. Then the market craters badly, resulting in sufficiently large losses that you decide to scale back your risk exposure on a go-forward basis. In both cases, personal experience drives your risk profile.

A sudden turn toward conservatism in your risk profile can cause a significant decline in your future wealth prospects. This concept is best described with an example. You have invested $1 million in the stock market, and then a foreign event (perhaps a war or a supply shock) tanks the market for a protracted period of time, resulting in your invested funds shrinking to a market value of $700,000. You decide to halt your losses, sell off your investments, and switch the resulting cash into a money market fund. This decision is likely caused by your sense of panic that a large part of your investment has been lost. By taking this step, you are certainly eliminating any further decline in your investments, but you have also sold out at the bottom of the market and stashed your cash in an investment vehicle that barely generates a return. A better approach (depending on the situation) might have been to control your sense of panic, wait out the stock market decline, and watch the value of your investments go right back up to where they had been before the financial crisis. To summarize, a good risk profile for an investor is being able to stick with your investments over the long haul, and not be overly concerned when their value dips from time to time.

In short, the best approach to managing your risk profile is – first – to recognize where your comfort level lies, and – second – to adjust your financial plan to match it. There is no point in trying to push the boundaries of your risk profile to the point where you are deeply uncomfortable with your investment strategy. Instead, just recognize your risk tolerance level, and work with whatever it may be. If you happen to have a low risk tolerance, then configure your financial plan to incorporate a lower rate of return on your investments – which may then require that you spend more time in the workforce or cut back on expenses in order to meet your financial goals.

We have just referred to the impact of emotions on your investment decisions – specifically, the sense of panic when your investments decline in value. There are actually several other emotion-related issues that can impact your investment decisions, which are as follows:

- *Historical loss avoidance.* If you have taken a significant loss on a particular investment in the past, you will be more likely to avoid that investment in the future – even though it has a good chance of spiking in value at some point in the future. For example, any crash in tech stocks inevitably leads some investors to leave in a huff, even though this sector has a strong record of generating quality returns over the long-term.

- *Over-confidence regarding expertise.* Many investors do not have a deep knowledge of investments, and yet consider themselves to be above-average investors. This feeling may be enhanced when their first investments turn out well. Overconfidence can lead to rash decisions to acquire riskier investments, which can lead to substantial losses during those inevitable periods when the economy sours or individual issuers experience financial troubles.

- *Over-reliance on recent history.* When you have generated unusually good investment returns recently, there is a tendency to more heavily rely on this recent history in making additional investment decisions – such as doubling down on the same investments. The reverse situation can also occur, where you might expect that recent declines in the market will continue into the future. Both of these assumptions can lead to the wrong investment behaviors, such as (in the first case) spending to acquire more investments in an over-heated market, or (in the second case) selling off investments in the depths of a stock market decline.

- *Sticking with familiar investments.* If you are comfortable putting your money into a specific investment, you are more likely to keep pouring funds into the same vehicle in the future, rather than diversifying your funds across a range of investments. This can result in an over-concentration of your wealth in a few investments, when a better approach would be to diversify across a broader range of assets. A common outcome of this situation is significant losses due to an over-concentration of invested funds.

It can be useful to be aware of these emotional issues, so that you can confront them as part of your wealth management activities. Being clear-eyed about how your emotions impact your investment decisions is crucial to making better decisions.

Another issue that impacts your risk profile is how you tend to use money. For example, you might be a miser, obsessively hoarding every penny. If so, you might need to consider whether it is reasonable to be overwhelmingly frugal, or if perhaps a loosening of the purse strings might be in order. Or, your use of money might lie at the opposite extreme, where you spend money obsessively, resulting in minimal cash reserves. If so, you might need to understand what spending restrictions will be required to generate some level of wealth. Another possibility is that you give away too much of your money, perhaps to other family members, friends, or charities. If so, you might need to consider setting up rules for capping the amount to be given away, so that you can build a reasonable amount of wealth. Yet another option is that you are excessively comfortable with risk, and so are willing to gamble on very risky investments in order to pursue a massive return – or a total loss. If so, you might need to set up rules for how much is to be invested in risky undertakings, in order to cap the amount at risk. Or, and preferably, you are motivated by the amount of cash you have piled up. This tendency leads to cost reduction and income building activities that increase your wealth over time. You should conduct some self-examination to determine which of these tendencies best describes you, and take steps to shift your tendencies more in the direction of an investor who is cognizant of his weak spots, and is willing to correct them.

Identify Your Investment Management Style

In addition to the preceding factors, it is also useful to understand your management style when it comes to investments. For example, you might be a complete do-it-your-selfer, covering all investment research on your own. In this situation, the intent is to achieve an investment return greater than the average rate of return for the market as a whole. This can involve shifting funds into asset classes that you think will outperform the market, as well as timing the market to purchase investments when prices are low[1]. This approach requires a substantial amount of time, especially if you have a broad range of investments or are active in swapping out investments on a regular basis. If so, you might need advice from an investment advisor for more complex investment strategies, especially ones that have complicated tax outcomes. In short, this investment style can be expensive and can take up a large part of your time, against which is offset the prospect of possibly generating outsized returns.

At the other extreme, you might choose to invest passively, where the goal is to simply match the rate of return for the market as a whole. This can be achieved by acquiring a representative sample of the target market's securities, or by buying into an index fund that tracks the market. This approach requires minimal time, and the associated costs are quite low. This is an excellent approach for those investors who have no interest in the day-to-day investment analysis grind.

A variation on these management styles is to invest a large part of your funds in passive investments (such as index funds), while reserving a smaller portion of your cash for more active investments, such as property, hedge funds, and emerging markets. This approach is useful when you want to limit the downside risk associated with more aggressive investments, while still preserving the possibility of significant upside gains.

Having a firm understanding of your investment management style will drive how you choose to spend your time in this area, and whether you should delegate investment-related activities to an advisor.

Note: The *efficient market hypothesis* states that the markets always incorporate all information, so it is impossible to beat the market. Thus, an investor would not be able to earn an outsized profit through the judicious selection of stocks, or by timing the purchase or sale of securities. Instead, the only way to earn an outsized profit would be to trade riskier securities. A logical outcome of this hypothesis is that you can generate reasonable returns simply by investing in a passive portfolio that carries a low overhead cost.

Summary

In short, wealth management begins with the ability to make rational investment decisions – about what you should invest in, how much to invest, and how long to hold it. This ability is based on a number of factors, including your life goals, risk profile, and investment management style. Only after you have thoroughly explored these issues will it be time to construct a financial plan for how to manage your wealth.

---

[1] Timing the market to achieve outsized gains is extraordinarily difficult, if not impossible. Market gains tend to come in short and unpredictable bursts. If you miss out on one of these gains, your overall returns will suffer significantly over the long term. A buy-and-hold strategy generates much better returns over the long term.

Chapter 2
The Financial Plan

Introduction

Once you have considered the topics listed in the preceding chapter, it is time to construct a preliminary financial plan. This plan begins with an itemization of your current financial position, and incorporates planning assumptions and several iterations of cash flow projections before you arrive at a viable financial plan.

Your Current Financial Position

A financial plan starts with a baseline, which is your current financial position. This should include a complete list of all significant assets and liabilities, as well as insurance policies and trusts. This itemization is needed in order to have a clear idea of the net amount of your assets, the returns generated from them, and any future changes to them (such as the cash surrender value of a whole life insurance policy).

In addition, itemize all sources of income, both now and in the future. For example, in addition to your current income, you might also expect pension payments once you reach the applicable age, as well as social security payments. It is useful to separately identify future sources of income that might not happen, such as an inheritance, since you may not want to lean too hard on these sources in your financial plan, in case they do not happen.

Liquidity Analysis

As part of your review of your current financial position, determine the liquidity level of your assets. An asset is considered to be liquid if it can be readily converted into cash. Thus, all cash deposits, money market funds, and securities that are routinely traded on an exchange are considered to be highly liquid. Illiquid assets are those that cannot be readily converted into cash, such as a residence, land, business investment, or investment fund with a long "lock in" period. It is easy to place an accurate market value on liquid assets, since there is a market price available for them. This is not the case with illiquid assets, for which it may be difficult to find a buyer on short notice, or at least at the price for which you would be willing to sell them. By having a clear understanding of which of your assets are *not* liquid, you can flag assets that may have a lower value than your stated estimate.

Liquid assets tend not to require ongoing maintenance costs, but this is not necessarily the case for illiquid assets. In particular, there can be substantial maintenance costs associated with property, including property taxes, repairs, and upgrades. When you itemize illiquid assets, be sure to include a reasonable estimate of these ongoing expenses (which may draw down your liquid assets when you pay for them).

> **Note:** Payments to maintain long-term assets are not necessarily a bad thing, since the returns from these assets may be quite substantial. Consequently, the presence of large ongoing maintenance costs should not necessarily drive the decision to sell off a long-term asset.

Investments in Private Businesses

It is especially difficult to evaluate an investment in a private business. On the one hand, these investments may pay out substantial dividends over time, representing an excellent return on investment. On the other hand, your share holdings in such a business are not registered, which means that you cannot sell the shares on a stock exchange; instead, it may be quite difficult to sell the shares. Also, these investments can vanish, since private businesses are generally smaller and more reliant on a relatively small group of customers, and so are at higher risk of bankruptcy than a large public company. For these reasons, it can be quite difficult to place a value on an investment in a private business.

Your Planning Assumptions

There are a number of assumptions that go into the formulation of a financial plan. One of the most important is how long you expect to live. While there may be inherited factors that will tend to cut short your life, it is likely that most people reaching age 65 will live into their mid-80s. The most fit individuals who also practice good eating habits can look forward to a life that may extend deep into their 90s. As a general rule, it is useful to assume that you will live until age 100. Since less than 1% of the population reaches that age, it is a good bet that a financial plan that provides for you through that age will be sufficient for your needs.

Another planning assumption is the amount of money that you plan to spend. This amount should be based on the hard reality of your current spending habits, adjusted for any expected changes once you retire. When in doubt regarding the amount of expenditures, try to somewhat overestimate the amount spent, to minimize the risk of running short at some point in the future. Also, include in this estimate the amount and rough timing of any capital expenditures (such as a new car or house), since these purchases can consume a large part of your assets.

> **Tip:** Be sure to factor in the cost of long-term care when compiling your expected costs. This can be a substantial sum, and may be incurred for a number of years.

In addition, include in your expenditure estimates a reasonable escalation to account for the effects of inflation. The long-term rate of inflation should form the basis for this estimate, with a heavier weighting for the historical inflation rate experienced over the past few years.

Another planning assumption is the use of a reasonable rate of return on investments. This rate should be conservative, and based on the mix of investments that you plan to hold during your retirement years. For example, you might switch from a 70/30 mix of equities and bonds at retirement to a more conservative 30/70 mix, which will likely result in a lower rate of return. The expected rate of return should certainly not exceed the historical rate of return, since a higher estimate would likely result in significant shortfalls from your planned returns on investment.

Yet another assumption is the presumed tax rate that is expected to apply to your income later in life. This may be a pure guesstimate, since politics can cause significant and unexpected swings in tax rates. Nonetheless, you should assume a reasonable rate, and certainly not one that is lower than the current tax rate.

These assumptions will have a profound impact on your financial plan. Be prudent in this area; being overly optimistic may result in a financial plan that is divorced from reality, and which might lead to a severe cash shortfall later in life.

The Cash Flow Projection

Your planning assumptions can be used to devise an initial cash flow projection for the rest of your life. This projection will certainly turn out to be incorrect in many respects, but it is useful for showing you the many factors that impact your wealth. This initial version is most useful for showing whether you will have the financial resources to attain your life goals.

Another use for the cash flow projection is for testing your assumptions. You can adjust each assumption for any number of issues to see how these changes impact your cash flows. For example, an assumption that a recently-discovered inherited genetic flaw might cut short your life by 10 years will certainly impact the plan. Or, an unexpected promotion with a large pay raise might have an inordinate impact on your projected cash inflows. Further, an expectation for a third child will trigger a re-evaluation of cash outflows to pay for this addition's living and educational expenses.

It can be useful to devise several cash flow projections. One version assumes that all of your savings will be exhausted during your lifetime, while another version assumes that your savings will be gone at about the time when you die, while a third version assumes that there will be substantial assets still remaining at your death. Any one of these analyses might prove to be correct, depending on variations in your income and expenditures over time, which in turn might be impacted by changes in the tax rate and inflation rate. You can keep updating these three models as the years pass, with all assumptions being changed to match your most recent experience. By taking this approach, you can be prepared for a worst case/most likely case/best case situation, and take steps as early as possible to adjust your lifestyle.

The main variable that can be adjusted for in a financial plan is your spending, since this is entirely under your control. Tax rates, investment returns, inflation, and even your own income are much less controllable (if at all), so you can routinely run plan updates with these other items updated in the plan, and then determine how the resulting changes will impact your spending plans.

Tip: Do not get too excited about short-term changes in your investment outcomes, since results can vary significantly over the long term. It is better to focus on the long-term average rate of return being generated. If you are concerned about a drop in a key assumption (such as the rate of return), just run the cash flow model more frequently, to see if a negative trend is developing. If you see a persistent trend over several iterations of the model, then it may be time to adjust your spending habits.

Plan Adjustments

The low/medium/high cash forecast is a good starting place for a financial plan, but it only incorporates a high level of cash inflows and outflows. It needs some fine-tuning to accommodate additional planning considerations. The first adjustment is for personal risks. For example, if there is a risk of a significant illness, then you might want to consider making an additional expenditure for long-term disability insurance. The reverse risk (if it can be called that) is of living too long, and outlasting your financial reserves. In this latter case, you might consider purchasing an annuity product that will provide you with an assured income for an extended period of time. Personal risk might also be extended to include the impact of your estate on those who will inherit it. If you are concerned about the amount that will be received, or about whether there will be enough cash to pay estate taxes, then consider purchasing life insurance that will be paid out to them after you die. You should also consider the need for insurance to compensate you for the loss of any illiquid assets, such as a home or a business. This is a particular concern when the assets are located in a higher-risk area, such as one that is prone to floods, wildfires, or earthquakes. There are costs associated with mitigating these risks, so those costs should be included in the expenditures portion of the financial plan.

Your Investment Strategy

You should adopt a specific approach to investment, rather than throwing money at the latest "hot" security. This should be laid out in a detailed strategy that states your investment goals, targeted rate of return, which assets are to be acquired for investment purposes, how much you intend to draw down from these investments each year (or add to them), and guidelines for periodically rebalancing your portfolio. This strategy document provides structure for your investment decisions, which can be important when you might otherwise be tempted to stray into a different investment direction. If you outsource the management of your investments to a professional manager, then he or she should use this strategy in managing your account. Several of the more popular investment strategies are noted in the following sub-sections.

Portfolio Rebalancing

An investment strategy typically states that you will be investing a certain proportion of your funds in particular asset classes, such as 60% in equities, 30% in municipal bonds, and 10% in emerging market securities. Over time, each of these asset classes will yield different rates of return, such as 8% for equities and 3% for municipal bonds.

Assuming that these returns are reinvested, the result will be a certain amount of portfolio drift, where some asset classes will expand beyond your target levels. When this happens, you should engage in *portfolio rebalancing*, selling some assets from those classes that have grown too large, and buying assets in those classes that are proportionally too small. The result is close adherence to your investment strategy.

An advantage of portfolio rebalancing is that you are forced to sell those asset classes at the point where their values are quite high, and use the proceeds to buy assets that have not been performing so well recently. In essence, you are selling at the high point for one asset and buying at the low point for another – which is a good way to obtain more assets at a reasonable price. This approach can be counter-intuitive to those investors who are attached to their high-flying assets, and see no reason to acquire under-performing ones. However, overpriced assets are more likely to drop in value, while underpriced ones are more likely to increase, so rebalancing is a good investment tool.

> **Tip:** There is no need to rebalance a portfolio too frequently. Ideally, you should rebalance when asset class valuations have drifted a modest amount, such as 10%, thereby reducing the amount of time and money required to sell and buy assets as part of the realignment.

Another way to rebalance a portfolio is to leave the overloaded asset classes alone, and just use any excess cash to buy more of the underperforming asset classes. To make this option work, you will need to turn off all dividend reinvestments for your existing equities, so that dividends will be paid to you in cash; these funds can then be used to acquire the necessary assets.

Tax-Loss Harvesting

Tax-loss harvesting involves the sale of securities at a loss in order to offset the amount of capital gains tax owed from the sale of profitable assets. For example, you have sold Security X and will have to pay tax on a gain of $50,000, so you sell Security Y (for which there is an offsetting loss of $50,000) in order to cancel out the gain with a loss. This tactic is used to limit the amount of tax that you would otherwise have to pay from the sale of assets. This approach is commonly used at the end of a tax year, which is a good time to assess your portfolio performance and its impact on your estimated taxes.

The Use of Leverage

Leverage is the use of debt to amplify your returns. This is done by taking on debt and using the borrowed funds to acquire assets that will (hopefully) generate a greater return than the cost of the debt. This can be a risky maneuver, especially when the cost of debt is high or the returns on the targeted assets are either in doubt or variable. In these cases, there is a good chance that you will lose money on this gambit. However, in cases where the cost of debt is extremely low and the returns to be made are locked in, then the use of leverage can be quite beneficial. For example, if you have access to a two-year loan at a fixed 2% interest rate, you could take on the loan and then use the funds to purchase a short-term bond with a fixed return of 3%, resulting in a net gain of 1% - and without even having to invest any of your own funds (though the lender might require some assets as collateral). While this might sound like an effective way to bolster your returns, just be sure to examine the characteristics of the debt to be taken on, the asset to be purchased, and any relevant tax laws to ensure that you can really achieve a positive return. Otherwise, you may be taking on a great deal of risk in exchange for a relatively small return.

Dollar-Cost Averaging

Dollar-cost averaging is an investment strategy where an investor contributes a fixed amount of money into a particular investment at regular intervals, regardless of the asset's price. This method aims to reduce the impact of market volatility by spreading purchases over time, rather than investing a lump sum all at once.

By consistently investing, this approach allows you to buy more shares when prices are low and fewer shares when prices are high. Over time, this can lead to a lower average cost per share compared to a one-time purchase made during a market peak. For example, if you put $500 into a mutual fund every month, you will accumulate more shares during market downturns and fewer during market rallies. This systematic approach can smooth out the effects of short-term price fluctuations and help mitigate the risks associated with market timing.

Dollar-cost averaging is particularly useful for long-term investors, such as those saving for retirement, because it encourages disciplined investing and emotional detachment from market swings. It also makes investing more accessible, as it requires smaller, consistent contributions rather than large lump sums.

However, dollar-cost averaging does not guarantee a profit or protect against a loss in declining markets. If the market experiences a prolonged downturn, the value of your investment may continue to fall. Additionally, during a rising market, a lump-sum investment made early may outperform dollar-cost averaging because more money is invested upfront and thus has longer to grow.

Despite its limitations, dollar-cost averaging is widely recommended for new and risk-averse investors who prefer a steady, predictable investment pattern. It promotes good financial habits, reduces the stress of market timing, and can be integrated into automated investment plans through employer-sponsored retirement accounts.

Sector Rotation

Sector rotation is an active investment strategy that involves shifting portfolio allocations among different industry sectors to capitalize on changing phases of the economic cycle. The core idea is that various sectors tend to outperform others depending on the macroeconomic environment – expansion, peak, contraction, or recovery.

During an economic expansion, cyclical sectors like technology, consumer discretionary, and industrials typically perform well due to increased consumer and business spending. As the economy reaches a peak and inflationary pressures rise, energy and materials often benefit from higher commodity prices. In a downturn or recession, investors may rotate into defensive sectors such as healthcare, utilities, and consumer staples, which tend to remain stable regardless of economic conditions. During a recovery, financials and real estate may lead as interest rates and credit activity begin to rise again.

Sector rotation requires careful analysis of macroeconomic indicators, such as GDP growth, interest rates, inflation trends, and employment data. Investors use this data to anticipate which sectors are likely to benefit in the next phase of the cycle. Exchange-traded funds and sector-specific mutual funds make implementing this strategy more accessible by providing exposure to entire sectors without the need to pick individual stocks.

While sector rotation can enhance returns and manage risk, it requires precise timing and a deep understanding of economic signals. Incorrect predictions about the economy's direction can lead to underperformance. It also involves more frequent trading, which may increase transaction costs and tax implications in taxable accounts.

Despite its complexity, sector rotation is a favored strategy among experienced investors who seek to outperform the broader market. When executed well, it allows investors to take advantage of macroeconomic trends and adjust their portfolios dynamically in response to changing conditions.

Summary

The key point to remember with a financial plan is that the first version of it is never the final one. You must regularly revisit the plan to determine how many factors have influenced it, such as changes in your income, rates of return, tax rates, and spending habits. If you persist in following your first financial plan for an extended period of time, there is a risk of failure – that changing circumstances will result in you running out of money at some point in the future. Therefore, always update the plan.

Chapter 3
Financial Advisors

Introduction

There can be significant problems associated with managing your investments by yourself. The typical person picks up financial information in a haphazard fashion, from a variety of sources. You might read stock tips on someone's blog, hear about the latest and greatest securities on a podcast, or perhaps learn about a new investment strategy at a cocktail party. These sources may not be reliable, since the people promulgating this information may have no formal background in investing at all. If you follow their advice, there is a good chance that your investing outcomes will be suboptimal, and possibly disastrous. A different option is to enter into a relationship with a financial advisor. In this chapter, we discuss the need for steady advice, the characteristics of an ideal advisor, and the fees they charge.

The Need for Steady Advice

The basic problem for many investors is that their news sources are fixated on the news of the day, which frequently involves slight incremental changes in well-known stock indexes, or changes in the prime interest rate. This focus does nothing to inform you about the true source of wealth, which is compounded returns on investment over an extended period of time. Your main focus should be on the reinvestment of dividends and interest to keep building your capital base over many years. By doing so, you can create several multiples of your original investment. For example, $10,000 invested at a 5% annual rate is worth $16,289 in 10 years, $26,533 in 20 years, $43,219 in 30 years, and $70,400 in 40 years. Or, stated differently, if you were to invest $10,000 at age 25, it would be worth more than seven times as much at your retirement at age 65. This is a boring strategy, but one that works exceedingly well.

But, rather than investing in a steady return and waiting for compounding to do its magic, the daily assault of financial news convinces you to try something else – perhaps investing in cryptocurrencies, or NFTs, or an investment fund that has reported outstanding gains over the past few years[2]. As a result, your funds are dragged through any number of investments, being whittled away by commissions and negative returns on investment, until you reach retirement age with little to show for it. This is where a financial advisor can be a useful source of steady advice.

A further use for a financial advisor is a periodic examination of whether you are withdrawing an appropriate amount from your investments each year. The advisor can model how your withdrawal rate will shrink your remaining investments over time,

---

[2] Fund managers go to great lengths to trumpet their historical returns, even though historical performance is not a valid indicator of future performance. The result is lots of investments in funds with sketchy investment strategies, resulting in significant losses.

which may result in a change in the withdrawal rate. This is an essential action to take at regular intervals, in order to keep from running out of money.

A financial advisor is certified in the field, is well-trained, and has lots of experience in providing financial advice. As such, an advisor can not only provide advice about how to handle your money, but also advice on where *not* to put it – the latter is especially useful when investors are flighty, constantly shifting among different investment options.

The Certified Financial Planner

The Certified Financial Planner (CFP) designation is a professional certification for financial planners that is conferred by the Certified Financial Planner Board of Standards in the United States, and by 25 other organizations that are affiliated with the Financial Planning Standard Board. This certification is usually considered the gold standard within the financial planning industry. To receive authorization to use the designation, a candidate must meet education, examination, experience, and ethics requirements, as well as pay an annual certification fee.

To initially certify as a CFP, a person must have a bachelor's degree (or higher), or its equivalent in any discipline, from an accredited college or university. As an initial step, students must learn a curriculum of about 100 topics pertaining to financial planning. Individuals holding professional designations that are pre-approved by the CFP Board, which include attorneys, certified public accountants, chartered certified accountants, chartered accountants, chartered wealth managers, chartered life underwriters, chartered financial consultants, and chartered financial analysts, are all allowed to take the examination without having to complete the education requirements. PhDs in business or economics are also exempted from the education requirements.

The CFP examination is a two-session affair that includes case studies, mini-case problem sets, and stand-alone questions that are used to assess an applicant's ability to apply his or her knowledge to financial planning situations. If an applicant passes the exam and meets all other requirements, then a CFP license is awarded. The applicant will then have to maintain his or her certification with an annual continuing professional education requirement that includes two hours of Board-approved ethics training.

Those who pass the exam must follow the CFP Board's code of ethics and professional responsibility, as well as the financial planning practice standard. The Board can enforce compliance with these standards via its disciplinary rules.

The Ideal Advisor

The ideal financial advisor is one who will conduct an in-depth assessment of your financial circumstances, develop a plan based on your life goals, and provide recommendations based on this document. The best advisors will also point out areas that you may have not considered, such as protecting family members in case of your demise. The ideal advisor will also provide you with a range of investment options, spending the time to explain the advantages and disadvantages of each one. You will have the option to make selections from this group, or not to select any of them – but the advisor should be able to put forward those products most likely to be of assistance to you, and in a cost-effective manner. Finally, the advisor should highlight any inconsistencies between your goals and the supporting financial plan, so that you can properly evaluate the options for bringing the plan into alignment with your goals.

It will be up to you to determine the frequency of interactions with a financial advisor. If you have a one-off issue, such as conducting a review of your pension situation, then it may be possible to get by with a single interaction. However, in cases where your tax situation is complex, or where you have a substantial amount of wealth, a better approach will be to have ongoing interactions with the advisor, where the advisor can make recommendations to adjust your investments to your changing circumstances. In the latter case, the advisor may be assisted by a group of experts who specialize in various aspects of your situation, such as pension, tax, trusts, life insurance, financial modeling, wealth transfers, charitable planning, and investment issues. The advice offered by this group may be fragmented and contradictory, so it is the responsibility of the financial advisor to develop a coordinated set of recommendations that will work for you.

> **Tip:** Some financial advisory firms attempt to augment their income by offering an annual advisory service – for a fee. This may not be necessary, if your financial circumstances rarely change. A more cost-effective approach may be to wait until there is a material change in your finances and then contact an advisor for advice.

A good financial advisor can also talk you through any number of life events, covering the financial impact of various decisions. For example, an advisor could offer advice for your spending on a child's wedding, whether to purchase a vacation home, whether to invest in a friend's business, and how to deal with the medical requirements of a parent. This might involve being a devil's advocate for a decision, or perhaps being someone who can expand on the financial ramifications of a decision. The advisor is also in an ideal position to steer you away from investment products that have been suggested to you by other parties, but which do not make sense for your specific situation.

The ideal financial advisor is someone who has been providing advice to you for a number of years. This person has likely acquired a substantial amount of experience with your family, including its quirks and unusual interactions, and so can provide nuanced advice that takes these factors into account.

Yet another skill of a good financial planner is providing you with a solid paper trail. This can be useful for dealing with taxes, where you may need (for example) to justify when charitable gifts were paid out, how they were valued, and whether the recipients were qualified from a tax perspective to receive the gifts.

Advisory Fees

Financial advisors can be compensated in a variety of ways. For example, they may be paid through ongoing service fees, such as $2,500 per quarter, or perhaps an hourly rate. Or, they may be paid a percentage of the assets under management, such as 2% of your assets per year. Or, if they are selling you financial products, they may receive a commission on each product sold. Depending on the situation, it is quite possible that an advisor will receive several of these types of compensation from you. Generally, the more complex financial products being sold will cost more than relatively generic ones.

> **Tip:** Insist on directly paying each advisory fee, rather than having it deducted from a financial product. Doing so ensures that you will be aware of the fees being paid. It is essential to see all fees, since they can offset a large part of your annual return on investments.

It always makes sense to compare the fees being paid to the level of value that you are receiving from an advisor. If you feel that an advisor is not providing value, then try someone else, or at least spread out the timing of scheduled meetings, so that fewer fees are being charged.

Advisor Evaluation Questions

When selecting a financial advisor, asking the following questions can be useful for determining which advisor will work best for you:

- Is your core service financial planning, or is this more of an adjunct to the sale of financial products?
- Are your financial products limited to a specific set of financial providers, or do you present offerings from the entire marketplace?
- What is the typical financial profile of one of your clients? Who is your ideal client?
- Do you provide a clear fee structure, so that I can see the amount I'm paying for each of your services? Do your fees include commissions on the sale of financial products? What is the minimum charge that I will incur?
- Who are the people I will be dealing with on an ongoing basis? Who will be my main point of contact?
- What are your professional qualifications, including certifications?
- Do you have in-house expertise in the wealth management areas that I need?
- What is your philosophy for investing client assets?
- What does one of your financial plans look like?
- What will be your approach to working with me to devise a financial plan?

These questions are useful for determining whether a financial advisor is properly equipped to service your needs, charges reasonable fees, and has a wealth management philosophy that aligns with your requirements.

Disadvantages of Using a Financial Advisor

While financial advisors can provide valuable guidance, there are several potential disadvantages to consider. Cost is a primary concern; advisors typically charge fees based on assets under management, hourly rates, or commissions. These costs can erode investment returns over time, especially if services are not tailored to your individual needs. Some advisors may also have conflicts of interest, particularly if they earn commissions from selling specific financial products, potentially leading to biased recommendations.

Another drawback is varying levels of expertise and credentials. Not all financial advisors are certified or held to fiduciary standards, which means they may not be legally obligated to act in the client's best interest. This can result in generic or suboptimal advice. Additionally, investors who rely too heavily on an advisor may become less engaged in their own financial education, leading to overdependence and reduced financial literacy.

Finally, there is the issue of limited personalization. Some advisors use standardized models that may not fully account for your unique goals, risk tolerance, or life changes. In such cases, a do-it-yourself investor who takes the time to learn may achieve better results at a lower cost. For these reasons, it is important to carefully vet any advisor before entering into a financial relationship.

Summary

It is not essential for everyone to have a financial advisor. However, it is more likely that you will need one if you have substantial wealth, must deal with a complicated tax environment, or have little experience with modeling financial outcomes. The key issue is recognizing when you are out of your depth, so that you can call upon someone who is trained in dealing with these issues.

Chapter 4
Wealth Preservation

Introduction

Wealth preservation involves investing your funds in such a manner that you are protected against the debilitating effects of inflation, while still maintaining a reasonable lifestyle. In this chapter, we cover investment principles, the concept of investment risk, and the primary types of investments.

Investment Principles

There are a few principles that can be of use in setting up a wealth preservation plan. By consistently following these principles, your chances of meeting your financial goals are improved. Here are some of the key principles to keep in mind:

- *Maintain adequate cash reserves*. Maintain a reserve of cash that is used to deal with short-term expenditures. The amount reserved in this manner should be sufficient to keep you from having to liquidate longer-term investments. The amount reserved in this manner does not have to cover every eventuality; it should be sufficient for your baseline monthly expenditure level, plus a reserve that will meet additional expenses likely to occur most of the time. Do not try to maintain a reserve so large that it will even cover unusual spikes in expenses, since doing so keeps the extra funds from being invested in something that might otherwise have generated a reasonable return on investment.
- *Diversify investments*. Do not invest in just a single asset, since a decline in its value could trigger a substantial decline in your invested capital. A better approach is to spread your investments across multiple *asset classes*[3], where each class is subject to different risks. Doing so reduces the risk that a single negative event will have an excessive impact on the value of your investments. You should spend a significant amount of time evaluating the risks to which each of your assets are subjected, and decide whether you are willing to accept those risks.
- *Avoid volatile investments*. Volatile investments are those that can generate inordinately high – or low – returns in any given period. When such an investment incurs a significant loss, it will require a great deal of growth in the future in order to make up for that loss. For example, a 50% drop in the value of an investment will require 100% growth in order to recover this loss, while

---

[3] An asset class is a grouping of investments that exhibit similar characteristics and are subject to the same laws and regulations. As an example of an asset class, equities exhibit high earnings but also high variations in the rate of return, and pay off in the form of dividends and asset appreciation. Another asset class is bonds, which provide reduced but more stable returns, and pay off in the form of interest payments.

a 10% drop in value would only have required 11.1% growth to recover the loss. The following exhibit shows the effect, where a volatile portfolio has to generate increasingly massive returns to offset a few losing years, just to match the return from a portfolio that earns a steady 7% return each year. Thus, building an investment portfolio with minimal volatility is an excellent way to assure long-term, steady growth.

- *Avoid taxes*. Income taxes can whittle down your returns, so invest through a tax-advantaged retirement account first, and try to hold stocks for a sufficiently long time to qualify any resulting gains for long-term capital gains tax treatment.
- *Minimize costs*. Minimize your trading fees by buying and holding stocks. Also, invest in funds where the management fees are low. Doing so can have a notably positive impact on your total investment return.

Above all, be calm. Do not sell in the midst of a massive market downturn, or be lured into investing in a "hot" sector, or buy when it seems that everyone else is piling into the market. Instead of following the herd, just devise an investment plan that works for you, and follow it consistently. It is easier to do this if you are not constantly monitoring the state of your investments. Instead, an end-of-month peek at the numbers should be more than enough for the long-term investor.

Comparison of Low-Volatility and High-Volatility Investments

	Low-Volatility Investment		High-Volatility Investment	
Year	Rate of Return	Ending Value	Rate of Return	Ending Value
		$100,000		$100,000
1	7%	107,000	20%	120,000
2	7%	114,490	-15%	102,000
3	7%	122,504	25%	127,500
4	7%	131,080	-15%	108,375
5	7%	**140,255**	30%	**140,888**

When these principles are consistently followed, your investment portfolio should be able to preserve its capital over the long term, while providing consistent returns on investment. This approach should also make wealth management more of a mechanical process, keeping you from bouncing among a variety of latest-and-greatest investment options.

Speculation and Investing

Speculation occurs when you make an investment that has a significant risk of loss, but for which there is also an expectation of a significant gain. Speculative activities focus on price fluctuations, where investors are more interested in generating a profit based on market value changes than on long-term investing. This can be done by acquiring assets just before they experience a run-up in value, or by selling them before the rest of the market sours on the investment. It is exceedingly difficult to time the market in this way, so investor results over the long-term tend to be less than what would be gained from a traditional investing philosophy, and could result in substantial capital losses.

A great many investors engage in speculation, which is the driving force behind investment bubbles. A bubble is caused when a large number of investors start to buy an asset, in the expectation that they are doing so before investors can jump in on the action; they can then profit from the resulting run-up in prices. While this may actually happen for a short period of time, the level of demand will eventually flatten out and then decline, resulting in a sudden and sharp reduction in the value of the asset – causing losses for those who did not exit the market at the right time.

Investment Risk

Investment risk is the probability of occurrence of losses relative to the expected return on an investment. Investment risk tends to be low for bonds, since any bond held to maturity will pay the coupon rate stated on the face of the bond document. Conversely, investment risk can be quite high for the shares issued by rapidly-growing startup companies, since the market price of these shares will vary substantially, based on changes in investor sentiment regarding how well the issuer will perform over time. In the latter case, there can be massive swings in the market price of the shares from the average price, so that you might lose money on the investment, or earn a stout profit. If you cannot stomach ongoing swings in investment valuation, then it is advisable to focus your investing activities on asset classes that experience minimal swings in valuation.

Your tolerance for investment risk may depend on the purpose of invested funds. For example, if you are setting aside money for your child's college education – which will commence in two years – then you will likely be quite conservative in investing the money, since you cannot afford to lose any of the investment. Conversely, if you are 25 years old and want to invest money for your own retirement (decades in the future) then it could make more sense to invest in asset classes that produce major swings in value – as long as their long-term trend is to provide an above-average return on investment.

Fixed Income Risk

Some investors park a significant amount of their cash in bonds, under the assumption that these investments yield relatively safe returns. This is not necessarily the case, for several reasons. First, bonds are not safe when the issuing entity has a low credit rating. These ratings are assigned by an independent credit rating agency, and are based on the financial and operational circumstances of the issuer. If the rating agency feels that an issuer has a poor probability of being able to pay back a bond, it assigns a "junk" credit rating to the bond. When these lower ratings are assigned, demand will drop for the associated bonds, so that they can be purchased for a lower price, resulting in a higher effective interest rate. However, this higher rate of return is coupled with a higher risk of default.

A second fixed income risk arises if you plan to sell your bond investment prior to its maturity date; when this is the case, any increase in the market interest rate will drop the market price of your bond holdings. Conversely, any decline in the market interest rate will increase the market price of your bond holdings. For example, you hold a bond that you purchased for $1,000, and which has a stated interest rate of 7%. However, the market interest rate subsequently increases to 8%. In order for an investor to earn this 8% rate on your bond, she would have to purchase it for $875 (calculated as $70 annual interest ÷ 8% interest rate). This means that, if you were to sell the bond now, you would incur a loss of $125 on the transaction. Or, you could continue to hold the bond until it reaches its maturity date, being paid 7% per year in interest, and then be paid $1,000 by the issuer when the bond is retired. Thus, shorter-term bond holding periods can result in some variability in returns, especially when interest rates are shifting rapidly.

There are several ways to reduce these risks. One is to only invest in highly-rated bonds, such as those carrying an investment grade of A through AAA. The issuers of these bonds maintain conservative financial positions, so their ratings are rarely downgraded. Conversely, this also means not investing in higher-yielding but lower-rated speculative bonds, for which credit rating downgrades are relatively common. Another risk reduction technique is to invest in bonds that will reach maturity within a relatively short period of time, such as within the next five years. When this is the case, there is less time during which movements in market interest rates can negatively impact the value of the bonds. When combined, both approaches can significantly reduce the risk related to bonds.

Tip: When market interest rates are very low, there is little room for interest rates to drop any further. In this situation, the only direction in which rates can go is upward, which will reduce the market value of your bond holdings. When this is the case, your best bond investment is in short-term bonds, which will not vary much in value until their maturity dates are reached.

When steps have been taken to eliminate fixed income risk, this presents the opportunity for you to accept greater risk in other parts of your portfolio, such as by pursuing higher-risk equities in emerging markets. In effect, you are spending your risk budget in other areas where the probability of a major payoff is higher. Thus, having a portion of your investments in minimal-risk fixed income securities gives you a steady source of returns, beyond which a tranche of funding can be used to pursue outsized gains in other asset classes.

Equity Risk

Equities have a long history of providing above-average returns, which can provide you with good protection from inflation over the long term. However, these returns can be quite volatile, with returns spiking in one year and plunging the next. This risk of reduced returns is heightened when you plan to invest in equities for only a few years, where just one bad year could crush your overall return on investment. Consequently, the best way to deal with equity risk is to commit to a long investment period, so that a few years of poor returns can be offset by a larger number of years with good returns.

Another way to deal with equity risk is to restrict the proportion of your funds invested in *emerging markets*. These are rapidly-developing countries with young populations and increasing living standards. While these factors might initially seem to be perfect for rapid gains in company value, there are also greater risks in these markets, especially when they are not stable democracies. In more autocratic countries, there is an enhanced risk of poor monetary policy causing a surge in inflation, as well as the sudden imposition of capital controls, and even of asset expropriation.

The Basic Investment Types

One of your key investment decisions is which types of investments to pursue – and which ones to avoid. In the following sub-sections, we note the general characteristics of the major investment types.

Ownership Investments

Taking an ownership stake in an investment tends to result in investment returns that are higher than the rate of inflation, resulting in above-average returns over the long term. Offsetting these returns are a higher risk of loss (since the investment vehicle may sometimes suffer major losses), as well as gyrating returns from year to year. However, if you can bear the risk of a potential loss of investment, taking an ownership interest can yield solid returns over the long term. The risk of loss can be reduced by diversifying your invested funds, to keep from putting all of your assets at risk.

Stock Market Investments

A common investment option is to buy the shares of publicly-held businesses. The prices of these shares are just as likely to decrease as to increase, so you may be in for a bumpy ride. If you do not want to invest too much in the shares of a single company, then another option is to buy a stock fund, which invests in clusters of shares. For example, a stock fund might invest in the shares of every stock issuer within a stock index, or only in the stocks of the technology sector, or only in the stocks of larger companies. These more dispersed holdings will shield you from large declines in the price of any individual stock, though doing so also prevents you from taking full advantage of a large run-up in the price of a single stock. Any of these investments can be made with an online brokerage account.

Generally, the way to make a reasonable return on stock market investments is to make investments in the market on a regular basis, keeping investing costs down, and restricting your investments to well-established businesses with a proven track record. Investing in startup companies is much riskier, since the chance of making a gigantic return is offset by the potential loss of your entire investment.

Real Estate Investments

Taking an ownership position in real estate presents the opportunity to not just profit from rent receipts, but also from the long-term appreciation of the property. Further, a large part of the funds used to invest in real estate comes from a mortgage, which means that the actual initial investment in real estate can be relatively small. This has proven to be a solid road to wealth for many investors. However, if you elect to manage properties directly (without a property manager), then real estate management can consume a large part of your time. In addition, it may be difficult to replace lost tenants, while older structures require substantial amounts of maintenance. Consequently, there is a risk that rental receipts will drop below expenditures, triggering losses. See our *Real Estate Investing* book for more information.

Business Ownership Investments

The most active type of ownership investment is in a business that you operate. The advantage here is that you have full control over how the business is operated, so the profits (or losses) generated are based on your decisions. This can result in significant cash flows from the business, as well as further profits from its eventual sale. A major downside of this approach is that a large part of your net worth may be tied up in the business, so if it fails, you might end up in a precarious financial position. See our *Entrepreneur's Guidebook* for more information.

Lending Arrangements

The largest alternative to ownership investments is to lend money to other parties. We do not refer to the issuance of actual loans, but rather to putting your money into savings instruments that yield a specific return. There are two variations on the concept, as noted next.

Savings Instruments

One of the safest investment choices is to invest in a savings instrument, such as a savings account at the local bank, or a certificate of deposit. Or, you may acquire a *bond*[4] that has been issued by a business or government entity. When you take this approach, you are essentially lending money to the savings institution or bond issuer. As a general rule, longer-term savings instruments pay back a somewhat higher interest rate than shorter-term instruments, though the difference in rates may not be that large.

There are pluses and minuses to the use of savings instruments. One plus is that these investments tend to be quite safe, and (depending on the circumstances) might even be guaranteed by the government. The main downside is the lack of any outsized returns. You will receive the interest guaranteed by the other party, but nothing more.

---

[4] A bond is a fixed obligation to pay that is issued by a corporation or government entity to investors. Bonds are used to raise cash for operational or infrastructure projects. They usually include a periodic coupon (interest) payment, and are paid off as of a specific maturity date.

For example, if Amazon issues a bond that pays 4% interest and you buy it, then you will receive a 4% return over the life of the bond – and nothing more. Meanwhile, Amazon may use your money to generate a 20% return, all of which benefits its shareholders. In addition, there is a risk that the rate of inflation over the term of the investment will exceed the return from it, in which case your actual return, net of inflation, will be negative. Furthermore (with the exception of interest on municipal bonds), you will also have to pay taxes on the interest earned, which reduces your return even more.

> **Tip:** If you *must* invest in a short-term savings instrument, then put the cash into a money market account. These accounts generate a higher return than your local bank, are easy to access when you need cash, and are quite safe. Their investments must have an average maturity of less than 60 days, which minimizes their sensitivity to changes in interest rates.

A key benefit of investing in bonds and other fixed-return instruments is that they lower investment risk by dampening the volatility of other investments, such as equities. However, the price of this risk mitigation is that the return on bonds is typically lower than for equities, so your long-term return on investment will decline as you put an increasing share of your funds into bonds.

Debt Reduction

An excellent investment choice can be to pay down existing debt. This is especially the case when the debt has a high interest rate associated with it, as is the case with credit card debt. Auto loans also tend to have relatively high interest rates associated with them, and so could be paid off in order to eliminate the interest payments. A variable-rate mortgage might also be a good choice for elimination, if the rate has escalated over time. A more problematic debt reduction is a fixed-rate mortgage, if the rate is relatively low. In this case, you might be able to gain a greater return from investing funds elsewhere, rather than paying down the mortgage.

Risk and Investing

The types of investing activities in which people engage is strongly influenced by their perception of risk. In many cases they place too much emphasis on avoiding lesser risks, while not doing enough to mitigate more substantial ones. In short, it is easy to misunderstand the impact of risk on your investments.

Part of the issues related to risk have to do with your sense of control over an investment. For example, you might have no concerns at all about spending $100,000 on new equipment for your business, because you are entirely in charge of the decision, and you have a very good idea of whether or not it will generate a return. Conversely, you might be petrified about paying $100,000 to purchase the bonds issued by a local city. The city might be in excellent financial condition, but your perception of risk is heightened because you have no control over the uses to which the city will put your money.

Despite these concerns, most people will take on investments that have some degree of risk associated with them, because the returns generated are generally higher. If they were to only put money into the safest investments, then the return on investment would be minimal. In short, there is a direct relationship between the risk of an investment and the return expected from it. In the following sub-sections, we discuss how to still generate reasonable returns while mitigating the associated risk.

<u>Mitigating the Risk of a Decline in Market Value</u>

It is not only possible but also quite likely that there will be a substantial drop in the stock market, perhaps due to a pandemic, war, or natural disaster. It is entirely possible for any funds invested in the stock market to experience an abrupt drop in value when one of these events occurs, perhaps in the range of 10 to 25 percent, though even larger drops have occurred. For example, the stock market crash of 1929 resulted in a 25% drop in the market over a span of just five days, while the financial crisis of 2008 triggered a 54% drop. Even though the stock markets are moderately well-regulated, it is still entirely possible that declines of this magnitude will occur again – and based on the historical evidence, they will almost certainly occur again.

One way to deal with a stock market decline is to view it as a buying opportunity. When stock prices decline, this is an excellent time to buy. If your budget routinely spins off more cash that can be invested, then consider investing it in the stock market in small amounts on a regular basis. By doing so, you can acquire shares at low prices even in the midst of a recession that will, in all probability, generate solid returns when the market eventually returns to normal.

The preceding recommendation should be accompanied by a note of caution. Do not buy stocks when they are clearly overpriced. While it is impossible to anticipate exactly when the stock market is about to drop precipitously, it is not difficult at all to identify overpriced stocks, simply by looking at a trend of their price/earnings ratios over time. In these situations, invest your additional cash in new investments that are not clearly overpriced. This might mean investing in foreign stock markets where prices are lower, or perhaps temporarily parking the funds in lower-return debt instruments until a market correction has occurred.

If you are in need of cash and you are holding some investments that are clearly overpriced, sell these investments first (subject to tax considerations). Doing so eliminates those investments that are most at risk of declining in value.

Another way to deal with a market decline is through diversification. Invest some of your cash in overseas markets, where the triggering event might not have as much of an impact. Or, invest a portion of the funds in real estate, or perhaps in bonds. By diversifying, only a portion of your funds will be at risk from any one event. It is quite possible that, while some investments are in decline, others will appreciate, resulting in a net overall gain.

Another consideration is your investment period. If you are willing to invest over a long period of time (such as several decades), then any short-term drops in the market – however large they may be – should not cause much angst. Over the long term, the market should recover from these declines, giving you a tidy return. If your expected holding period covers a shorter period of time (as is the case for someone nearing retirement), then it might be prudent to gradually shift your funds into more stable investments, such as bonds, so that you won't have to worry about sudden drops in value. Shifting to more stable returns will likely result in lower returns, so there is a cost associated with taking this approach.

> **Tip:** If you are uncertain about how you would feel about buying into risky investments, then consider making a small investment of this type, and monitor how you feel about it over time, as its value spikes and plunges. This will help you to understand whether a larger investment is warranted – or none at all.

Mitigating the Risk of a Decline in a Specific Investment

If you have poured your funds into a relatively small number of investments, then a decline in the value of any one of them will have a disproportionately large (and negative) impact on your total holdings. The obvious mitigation activity in these cases is to diversify into a broader range of investments. For example, if your funds are concentrated in technology stocks, consider shifting some of it to unrelated industries, such as hotels or mining. Doing so makes it less likely that an industry-wide decline will have a severe impact on your holdings.

A good way to diversify is to hire a professional to do it for you. A professional manager has a better understanding of the risks associated with investments, and knows which companies in various industries represent a good value. The fees charged for this service are well worth the resulting risk mitigation.

If your investments are concentrated in real estate, then be sure to conduct detailed due diligence on all properties that you are considering buying. This means not taking any shortcuts on inspections. A few pennies saved up front on inspections can be extremely costly over the long term, if they result in you not knowing about issues that have to be repaired at a later date.

Mitigating the Risk of Inflation

A major concern is the negative impact of inflation on your investment returns. It is entirely likely that even a modest rate of inflation will completely offset any returns generated by low-risk investments (such as government bonds). To keep this from happening, allocate a reasonable proportion of your investable funds into higher-return (and yes, riskier) investments; doing so will generate returns sufficiently high to offset the negative effects of inflation.

FDIC Coverage

We leave this section with a brief discussion of the benefits of FDIC deposit insurance coverage. The Federal Deposit Insurance Corporation (FDIC) is an independent agency created by Congress to maintain stability and public confidence in the nation's financial system. Among other functions, the FDIC insures bank deposits, so that you will not lose deposited funds in the event of a bank failure. The standard insurance amount is $250,000 per depositor, per insured bank, for each account ownership category. If you open a deposit account in an FDIC-insured bank, you are automatically covered.

What this means is that, if you insist on keeping funds in a bank, rather than in some more productive investment vehicle, then be sure to cap your deposits at each bank at $250,000. Any funds over that amount will not be insured by the FDIC. This can result in having a number of accounts scattered across several banks.

Summary

In this chapter, we discussed the risk/return tradeoff, and how you need to allocate your funds among a variety of asset classes in order to mitigate your risk level. A concentration of your wealth within a single asset class can be quite risky, especially when that asset class has a history of generating volatile returns. In short, the key to preserving your wealth is to spread out your investments among a variety of unrelated asset classes, while being knowledgeable about the investment risks associated with each one.

Chapter 5
Investing in Stocks

Introduction

In this chapter, we cover the essentials of investing in stocks, including how to conduct research, types of investing strategies, and investing best practices. We also cover the business activities and types of information that can move stock prices. The advice provided in this chapter is critical for the development of a coherent long-term strategy for investing in stocks.

How Businesses Raise Money

Before we discuss investing in stocks, it may be worthwhile to briefly discuss how businesses raise money. An organization may sometimes need extra cash to expand its operations, invest in new products, or build its working capital in order to fund more inventory and receivables. The best fundraising route for a small business is through a loan from the local bank, but the options expand considerably for larger firms. One option is to sell bonds to investors. A bond is classified as debt, since the issuer promises to repay the bond on its maturity date, and also makes regular interest payments to investors. Companies are more likely to issue bonds when the market interest rate is low, and especially when the share price is low (meaning that the owners would have to give up a large ownership interest in the company in order to raise a sufficient amount of money).

The other fundraising option is to sell shares in the business. Once sold to investors, these shares can be traded on a stock exchange, allowing investors to readily liquidate their investments. An issuer is not required to buy back shares, though some companies occasionally do so. Instead, investors make money from periodic dividend payments, as well as from any appreciation in the price of the shares on the stock market. A share issuance is a good choice for a rapidly growing company that needs a large amount of funding, and does not have the cash flow to buy back bonds from investors. It is also a good idea when the stock market is peaking, or when market interest rates are so high that bond financing would be too expensive. The primary downside to selling shares to the public is the onerous reporting requirements associated with doing so, which can be quite burdensome – especially for smaller businesses that do not have the financial resources to pay for these activities.

How Businesses Add Value

When companies sell shares to the public, their investors want to experience some price appreciation in their holdings. This happens when demand for those shares increases, which is triggered by either reporting higher profits or the anticipation of higher profits in the future. Therefore, to meet shareholder demand for higher share prices, a business may engage in any (or all) of the following activities:

- *Add markets*. One of the easier ways to increase profits is to increase the number of markets in which a company's goods are sold. For example, a company that manufactures furniture could begin by selling its products in just one state, and then within the surrounding states, then nationwide, and then internationally. However, these expansions can increase the complexity of operating the business, and may require the use of partners to assist in selling, which tends to reduce profits. In addition, products may require some modification to be successful in foreign markets, which can also impact profits.
- *Build a brand*. A business can invest heavily in advertising and product quality in order to increase brand recognition. This can allow a business to increase its prices, though the brand-building exercise does not always succeed, and must be reinforced over time with additional expenditures.
- *Control costs*. Any business needs to maintain tight control over its cost structure. This must be done carefully, so that cost reductions do not impact the quality of a company's products. Cost control can be something of a minefield for businesses that are also building brand recognition, since branding requires major expenditures, and mandates that a high level of product quality be maintained.
- *Enter adjacent markets*. If a company's current market niche has been largely exploited, then a logical next step is to enter adjacent markets where it can take advantage of its existing expertise. For example, a garden products company could expand into lawn care, while a manufacturer of automobiles could expand into the production of trucks. This approach can be difficult, since some additional expertise must be acquired when entering adjacent markets.
- *Invest in new product development*. When the investment community sees that a business is rolling out new products that can increase its sales and profits, demand for its shares will increase. However, this is not an easy path to follow. The business must be able to convert its research efforts into workable products that beat the offerings of competitors, and without excessively cannibalizing sales of the firm's existing products. In short, new product development must be carefully managed.
- *Pursue niches*. A potentially very profitable approach is to find underserved niches in the market and fill the needs of those customers. This may involve a significant repositioning of the company, perhaps with specially-designed products, different customer service, and so forth. If done successfully, customers may be willing to pay higher prices for the firm's goods and services.

The job of the investor, or the investor's advisors, is to monitor how well companies are pursuing these strategies, and to invest in those whose efforts appear most likely to generate outsized profits. It also means selling off the shares of those entities whose strategies appear to be failing or at least underperforming. This is very much a forward-looking effort, since other investors are also engaged in this research, and their collective opinion of the prospects of a business is reflected in the current market price.

Characteristics of Stocks

A *stock* is a security that represents the ownership of a fraction of a corporation. This ownership interest entitles the owner to a proportion of the firm's assets and profits. Units of stock are called *shares*. Stock ownership is a good way for investors to share in the wealth generated by businesses, since the historical rate of return on these investments has exceeded the rate of inflation.

There are two ways in which an investor can earn a return on stock holdings. One is through dividend payments. A *dividend* is a payment to shareholders of a portion of a corporation's earnings. The amount to be paid is decided by the organization's board of directors. The payment is nearly always in cash, but can also take the form of property or additional shares of stock. Larger companies are more likely to pay dividends, because they have a stable stream of income from which to make payments. Smaller, rapidly-growing businesses need every penny they can get to fund their growth, and so are much less likely to pay dividends.

> **Tip:** If you do not need the cash from dividends, by all means reinvestment them in order to maximize the benefit from compounding. Over the long-term, this can result in a substantial increase in your returns.

The other way for investors to earn a return is via increases in the price of their stock holdings. When this happens and investors want to pocket the proceeds, they sell the shares on a stock exchange, thereby converting the shares into cash. It is also entirely possible that share prices will decline, in which case selling them will result in a loss for an investor.

The Stock Market

When we refer to the *stock market*, we are talking about the collection of exchanges at which the shares of publicly-traded companies are bought and sold. These transactions are conducted through physical or electronic exchanges, or through the over-the-counter market (which operates under different rules). There are many stock exchanges, including the New York Stock Exchange, the NASDAQ, and the Tokyo Stock Exchange.

In brief, stock exchanges provide a secure and (very) regulated environment in which to buy and sell financial instruments, with minimal operational risk. An exchange can act is a primary market, where a company conducts an initial public offering, selling its shares for the first time to investors. Or (and more commonly), it acts as a secondary exchange, where investors buy and sell shares amongst themselves. Issuing companies directly benefit from the cash received from primary markets, while their investors benefit from the secondary exchange role. In either role, a stock exchange facilitates transactions, and is paid a fee for doing so.

Stock exchanges operating within the United States are monitored by the Securities and Exchange Commission (SEC). The SEC also protects the investing public by promoting the full disclosure of financial information, as well as by investigating cases of financial fraud. In addition, the SEC specifies the reporting requirements of all publicly-held entities within the country, and makes their filings available to the general public on its website.

Investors commonly track the overall trend of stock valuations within the stock market with one or more stock indexes. A *stock index* is a group of shares that are used to give an indication of the stock market as a whole or a subset of it. A good index to use that reasonably represents the performance of the stock market as a whole is the Standard & Poor's 500 Index. It contains 500 companies based in the United States, which represent about 80% of the total value of the stock market. A more comprehensive index is the Wilshire 5000, which includes all publicly-traded companies with headquarters in the United States. The NASDAQ Composite Index is derived from more than 3,000 stocks that are listed on the NASDAQ stock exchange. Since the NASDAQ lists the stocks of a disproportionate share of technology companies, it tends to be more representative of the performance of that sector.

Perhaps the most commonly-cited index is the Dow Jones Industrial Average (DJIA), which includes the stocks of 30 large companies that are based in the United States. The DJIA represents about 25% of the value of the stock market. However, since the DJIA only contains the stocks of very large companies, it does not necessarily represent investor opinions regarding the rest of the market.

The main use of stock indexes is to give you a quick view of the direction in which the market is heading, which is a gauge of investor sentiment. These indexes can also be used to compare the performance of a single stock to a representation of the market as a whole, to see if it is underperforming or overperforming.

Market Moving Events

Financial markets tend to be quite efficient, because there are many buyers and sellers, and they all have access to approximately the same information. Consequently, only new information that the investment community has not yet seen should impact the markets to a significant extent. Market prices move a lot, so clearly a great deal of information is constantly impacting the markets. What types of information have the most immediate impact on the market? Here are some pointers:

- *Earnings reports.* Publicly-held companies are required to issue their financial results once a quarter, and their annual results following the end of each fiscal year. In addition, they may hold earnings calls, which are conference calls in which they clarify the information presented in their financial statements. When several companies in an industry sector report unusually high or low earnings, this is a signal to investors that the economy is changing. For example, a cluster of low earnings reports is a strong signal that the economy is cresting, and may be about to head into a recession.

- *Economic indicators.* An *economic indicator* is economic data used to interpret the current or future state of the economy. Investors are especially interested in leading indicators, which predict future economic activity levels. Examples of leading indicators are the number of new building permits, surveys of consumer sentiment, and new orders for manufacturers. The release of leading indicators to the public can definitely deliver a jolt to the financial markets – in either direction.

- *Interest rates*. The stock market goes up when interest rates decline, and reverses direction when interest rates increase. The reason is that heightened interest rates increase borrowing costs, which tends to contract economic activity, driving down profits. Also, when interest rates increase, investor money tends to shift out of the stock market and into bonds and other debt instruments. Conversely, when interest rates are low, investors shift their money out of bonds and back into the stock market, which drives up prices.

- *Political changes*. The markets will react when a different political party or politician takes over a country. This represents a change in continuity, which can alter the underlying economics of a country. For example, when a socialist-leaning government is replaced by a free-market government, the financial markets are likely to jump up, on the expectation that taxes and trade barriers will be lowered, resulting in more corporate profits.

- *Supply and demand*. Changes in supply and demand can definitely impact the financial markets. For example, when there is a constriction in the supply of key goods, such as computer chips, this constricts the sales of downstream products that use computer chips, resulting in reduced sales and profits. Conversely, the opening of a major new computer chip factory has the reverse impact, since it tends to expand sales of downstream products.

- *Wars*. Markets tend to drop when a war starts, because borders are closed, making it more difficult to transport goods across borders. A minor war in a distant region is unlikely to have much of an impact, but a major one may send the markets into a tail spin. These conflicts will have varying impacts on individual companies, however. For example, a war in Ethiopia would tank the stocks of any coffee plantations in the area whose production will be impacted, but will raise the stock prices of competitors located elsewhere, which will benefit from the reduced level of coffee supply.

Bull Markets and Bear Markets

A *bull market* occurs when asset prices rise at least 20% over a sustained period of time. Conversely, a *bear market* is one in which asset prices fall by at least 20% over a period of at least two months. Markets tend to go through these periods of boom and bust, with durations lasting from a few months to many years. There can also be extended periods between bull or bear markets, where prices meander about with no clear upward or downward direction.

Bull markets are typically associated with a growing economy, low unemployment, and high investor confidence, where increasing corporate profits trigger increasing stock prices. The prospect of even higher reported profits in the future incentivizes investors to keep bidding up stock prices, until the economy tops out. At this point, there is a risk of a bubble, where stock prices exceed the underlying fundamentals of corporations. Stock prices then fall – perhaps quite dramatically – which may trigger the onset of a bear market.

It can be quite difficult to anticipate when a bull or bear market will begin or end, so many investors elect to leave their asset allocations alone over the long term, allowing their asset values to rise and fall as each successive bull or bear market occurs. Other investors will try to anticipate these shifts, and will alter their mix of asset holdings accordingly.

Investing Strategies

The traditional investing strategies have been the growth, value, and income approaches, which are described first in the following bullet points. We follow those strategies with a number of more specialized techniques, such as ones relating to expected or rumored merger activity. Also, high frequency trading comprises a large part of all trades in a company's securities, though it is not based on a long-term investment strategy. The most common approaches to investing are as follows:

- *Growth strategy.* Some investors buy shares of companies in their early stages of development, on the assumption that these businesses will ramp up quickly and experience high rates of revenue growth. They then sell their shares once a company's fundamentals appear to be maturing, with lower growth rates and a steady proportion of market share. These investors are particularly focused on the rate of growth of a company's revenues and earnings per share, as well as the speed with which they are growing in comparison to the rest of the industry. Once a business reports a slower rate of growth, expect these types of investors to sell out, which may put downward pressure on the stock price.

- *Value strategy.* Some investors will only buy stock when it is trading at multiples notably lower than those of the industry at large. They will hold the shares until such time as they believe the shares have returned to the industry average, and then sell the shares. These investors are most interested in the ratio of a company's share price to its book value, which they will compare to the same ratio for other companies in the same industry. In addition, they delve into the basic earnings fundamentals of a business, to ensure that the current low valuation is not caused by financial issues that could derail their investment. Also, they are more likely to buy a company's shares shortly after it declares a profit warning, since the warning probably triggers a price decline. An interesting side effect of having value investors is that their purchasing activities tend to keep a share price from dropping too low, while their planned selling tends to keep share prices from rising too high. Thus, value investors tend to have a moderating influence on stock price volatility.

- *Income strategy.* Some investors are only concerned with the dividend payments they receive from their investments. The issuance of a continuing series of dividends will attract this group of investors, and they will leave immediately if a company reduces, delays, or eliminates its dividend. These investors are most interested in an uninterrupted history of dividends, a continuing increase in the dividend amount paid per share, and enough information about the fundamentals of the business to gain assurance that the dividend will not be reduced.

- *Growth at a reasonable price.* Some investors are positioned midway between the growth and value strategies. They buy shares when the current market valuation of a business appears inordinately low, but only in conjunction with a reasonable prospect for future growth. They will still sell their shares when a company's valuation has reached a certain point in relation to the industry average, but may also retain their holdings somewhat longer if the prospect of additional revenue growth appears to warrant the risk of retention.

- *High frequency trading.* The majority of all securities trades are now initiated by entities that engage in high frequency trading. These firms are essentially market makers, since they buy shares from sellers at the bid price, and then sell the shares to other investors at the offer price a few moments later, earning a fraction of a cent per share. This can be called an investing strategy, since the traders are buying and selling – they are just not holding shares for very long. Clearly, these investors have no interest in the financial condition of a company whose shares they are trading.

- *Technical analysis strategy.* Some investors are extremely active with their investments, closely tracking the historical behavior of stock prices and using this information to estimate where stock prices will be in the very near future. One of the more popular versions of technical analysis is momentum investing, which is the theory that securities that have done well in the recent past will continue to do so in the near future. These investors have only a moderate interest in a company's fundamentals, since they are moving in and out of investment positions on a continual basis.

- *Merger arbitrage strategy.* Investors buy the shares of companies that they believe will be acquired, and profit from the eventual (and presumably higher) price at which acquisitions are completed. This strategy can result in massive surges and declines in stock volume as acquisition rumors ebb and flow.

- *Roll up strategy.* There are rare cases where a company is unusually good at acquiring and wringing excellent results out of other businesses. Investors look for a continuing history of acquisitions that routinely result in accretive increases in earnings. They buy shares in acquiring businesses that show accretive earnings, in hopes that the gradual accumulation of purchasing power and other advantages by the acquirer will yield outsized earnings, and therefore sharp increases in the stock price.

- *Theme investment strategy.* Some investors prefer to obtain deep knowledge about a particular industry or commodity, and only invest in those areas. For example, an investor may choose to invest solely in the automobile manufacturing market. As another example, an investor may be an expert on the impact of changes in the price of copper on many industries, and chooses investments based on those impacts. These investors are less concerned with the fundamental profitability of a specific business; instead, they tend to buy or sell the shares of clusters of similar companies.

Note the different types of information that growth and value investors use. Growth investors are most concerned with the information appearing on a company's income statement, while value investors are more concerned with the book value information appearing on the balance sheet. A technical investor or a theme investor has less interest in either information source.

The following bullet points do not describe additional investment strategies; instead, they address the circumstances under which a person comes into the ownership of company shares. These sometimes-inadvertent investors may have no real strategy for what to do with the stock. Where possible, we have noted their possible reactions to stock ownership. The "strategies" are:

- *Company employees.* Some people own shares in a business simply because they happen to be employees of the company. The company may have issued shares to them as part of an initial public offering, or for other reasons. These shares are likely to be initially restricted, with a waiting period and other requirements being imposed before they can be sold. Not all employees are financially sophisticated, and their shareholdings may also be extremely small. For both reasons, there tends to not be much activity in these shares. If anything, company employees tend to forget that they even *own* the shares. If employees do remember their shareholdings, they are more likely to retain them out of loyalty to the company.

- *Inheritance.* An individual may inherit shares. If so, there are two possible outcomes. One is that the recipient is barely aware of the shares (usually when the shareholding is quite minor), in which case the shares are unlikely to be traded. The other outcome is that the recipient is financially sophisticated, and will immediately roll the shares into his or her portfolio; if the shares do not match the person's investment strategy, they will be sold.

- *Stock options.* Members of the management team, and sometimes other employees that a business wants to retain will be issued stock options, under which they have the option to purchase company shares at a certain price within a specific date range. Any shares purchased under a stock option plan are likely to be restricted, and so will not be traded for some time. However, the recipients of shares purchased under stock option plans will face a tax burden from their earnings, and so will likely sell at least some of these shares as soon as possible in order to generate enough cash to pay their tax obligations. Thus, an exercised stock option will likely lead to the sale of a portion of the related shares as soon as they become unrestricted.

- *Stock purchase plans.* Some companies offer stock purchase plans to their employees, under which the employees can buy shares through ongoing payroll deductions, and usually at a discount to the market price. Participants in stock purchase plans tend to be somewhat more financially sophisticated, and so will be more likely to sell their shares at the right price.

This last group of points indicates that the circumstances under which shareholders come by their shares can have an impact on their propensity to hold or sell the shares.

Mutual Funds

Thus far, we have assumed that investors want to purchase the shares of particular companies. What if this is not the case? You might not want to spend the time required to research companies. If so, a mutual fund might be a better approach to investing. A *mutual fund* is a type of financial vehicle that is made up of a pool of money obtained from a large number of investors; its goal is to invest the money in a variety of securities, as stated in its prospectus. The money is invested by a group of professional money managers. Any gains or losses are allocated proportionally among the investors. Investing in a mutual fund is a good option for investors that do not have enough time to conduct their own investment research. A further advantage is that the fund's holdings can be diversified across many assets, thereby reducing the likelihood of suffering significant losses. The main downside to these funds is that the fund manager decides when to sell assets, which can result in taxable distributions at inopportune moments.

A variation on the mutual fund concept is the *exchange-traded fund* (ETF), which invests in a particular index, industry, or commodity. It is easy to invest in an ETF, since it is traded on a stock exchange. The operating expenses of an ETF that follows an index are especially low, since there are no investment decisions to be made.

A Word on Speculative Bubbles

It is all too easy for investors to be sucked into *speculative bubbles*, which are spikes in asset values that are fueled by irrational speculative activity that is not supported by the fundamentals. These situations arise when someone who bought in at a low price promotes the idea that a security is bound to increase in value, which in turn brings in more investors who also promote it, in hopes of a further rise in value. This "piling on" effect does indeed keep raising the price, but eventually there are no more new investors willing to buy, at which point demand falls, triggering a steep decline in the price – and many investor losses.

There are a few general rules to follow to avoid speculative bubbles. First, always look at the fundamentals. For example, if the price/earnings ratio has been trending up steeply, then it is already too late to buy a security. Or, if the underlying business is not generating positive cash flow, then there is no basis for a high stock price valuation. Second, look at the metrics being cited. If someone has developed a new investing metric to justify a high valuation, such as a revenue to stock price multiple instead of the usual price/earnings ratio, then be very suspicious. Third, if short sellers are betting heavily against the company, there is probably a good reason for it. Short sellers dig through a company's financials for signs of problems, and will sell short in the expectation of a future drop in the stock price.

When it is apparent that a speculative bubble is building, this is a good time to park your excess cash in a money market account and wait for the bubble to burst. When stock prices have dropped in the aftermath of the crash, swoop in with your excess funds and buy shares at their new "value" prices.

> **Tip:** As the global population continues to expand into every corner of the globe, the amount of infrastructure required to support it must also expand – which means that a hiccup anywhere in the system can cause major problems for the world economy at any time. That being the case, it is likely that the next hiccup – whatever it is – is probably only a few years away. Therefore, maintain a good reserve of cash for the inevitable stock market downturns associated with these events, and get ready to buy on the downturn.

Penny Stock Concerns

A variation on the speculative bubble to guard against is anyone pushing penny stocks. A *penny stock* refers to a small company's stock that trades for less than $5 per share, and which trades over-the-counter, rather than through a stock exchange. These stocks trade at such low volumes that it is easy to manipulate their share prices. For example, a brokerage could assign one of these penny stocks to its sales staff, who call likely prospects to drum up interest in it. They typically tout the stock as being about to take off in price, which means that buying it right now at a bargain price of $___ will assure gargantuan profits down the road. The usual outcome is that the brokerage sells the stock at an inflated price, pockets a large profit, and then leaves the investors to suffer losses as the stock price declines back to where it was before the brokerage got involved. In short, when someone calls you with such a sales pitch, hang up. The same advice applies to any other form of investment-related communication.

A Word on Money Manager Performance

There are thousands of money managers out there, all scrambling to manage your funds. They promise market-beating performance in exchange for a fee – and that fee can be substantial. So, are money managers worth their cost? Over the short term, some money managers are bound to outperform the market, due to a mix of lucky asset picks and the subsequent performance of those assets. The problem is that these few managers cannot persistently replicate this performance. Instead, their performance drops, while other money managers have a lucky year or two, and rise above the pack. This presents a problem for the investor, who wants to select a money manager at the start of one of these lucky runs. The problem is contained within the word "lucky," which is defined as "having good things happen to you by chance." In essence, even picking the right manager is lucky; so over the long run, it is not possible to consistently pick money managers who will deliver market-beating performance for you.

The lesson to be learned here is that money managers might possibly deliver a short-term performance boost for you, but cannot do so over the long term. In exchange for this "service," they (quite reliably) charge service fees that are likely to reduce your investment returns to a level below what is being generated by the market as a whole. These service fees will take a substantial bite out of your long-term returns, resulting in your nest egg having a much lower value over the long term.

How to Judge Your Investing Performance

All too many investors want to see immediate improvements in the value of their stock portfolios. If they do not see increases within a few months – or even weeks – then they sell their holdings and try something else. This is most unwise, since the valuation of your portfolio will fluctuate over an extended period of time. For example, there may be two or three years of moderately steady increases, followed by a sharp decline, followed by a few years of variable outcomes. How you judge the performance of the portfolio depends on when you acquired stocks during this series of events. A better approach is to monitor portfolio performance over a much longer period of time, such as five to 10 years. By doing so, you will be less inclined to continually swap out stocks, which in turn minimizes sales commissions. A further advantage is that holding stocks for longer periods of time qualifies any gains to be taxed at the much lower long-term capital gains rate. Conversely, if you constantly buy and sell shares, then any gains on a stock held for less than one year would be taxed at the higher short-term rate. A final advantage of only measuring your performance over the long term is that it ensures that you have money invested in the stock market at all times – which positions your money perfectly to benefit from unexpected jumps in stock prices. If you had instead been jumping in and out of the market, there is a good chance that you would miss one of the run-ups in price.

In short, stocks are intended to be long-term investments, so only measure their performance over the long term. Any shorter investment interval can result in adverse investing behavior that reduces your return on investment.

Summary

We have noted a variety of investing strategies in this chapter, along with how to collect more information to support whichever approach you prefer. Even more important are the concepts of developing a diverse portfolio and of investing over the long term. Though it is possible to win big from a single investment, a much more prudent approach is to spread your money among a range of unrelated investments, so that a loss on any one investment will have only a modest impact on your returns. And, be aware that the best returns only occur over the long term. This means sticking with your investments for years, rather than constantly churning your portfolio. These two principles make it much more likely that your investing activities will bear fruit.

Chapter 6
Investing in Lending Arrangements

Introduction

There are several types of lending arrangements in which investments can be made, such as savings accounts, certificates of deposit, and bonds. Under these arrangements, you essentially lend money to the recipient in exchange for what is usually a fixed payment – there is no upside potential for additional payments, nor is there any resulting ownership in the recipient entity. In this chapter, we cover the characteristics of lending arrangements and how to buy bonds.

Characteristics of Lending Arrangements

The main benefit of any lending arrangement is a steady stream of interest payments from the borrower. This is not a minor issue, since it can provide some income stability, especially when the bulk of your assets are parked in more volatile equity investments that may not make any periodic payments, and which might even decline in value over time. This level of stability and income makes lending arrangements a good choice for investors who need some ongoing income, and especially so when the prospect of investment volatility makes it difficult for them to sleep at night.

Balanced against these benefits is the lower return on lending arrangements, which can make it difficult to attain any net return after the negative effects of inflation are considered. Furthermore, investing in these instruments means that you are not using the money to invest in higher-return stocks or real estate, so the opportunity cost of lending arrangements can be substantial.

Lending Choices

The main lending choices are products offered by banks, money market funds, and bonds. In the following sub-sections, we cover all of these topics and pay particular attention to the different types of bonds and their features.

Banks

Banks offer both savings accounts and certificates of deposit. Savings accounts pay a minor interest rate and allow for immediate withdrawals, while certificates of deposit pay a somewhat higher rate, but in exchange for not being able to withdraw the cash early (or at least not without having to pay a fee). The interest paid by banks is usually quite low, because they must also pay for their operating costs – which can be substantial. A benefit of parking money in a bank is the $250,000 account insurance provided by the federal government. However, the interest rates offered are painfully low, so it can make sense to explore other options.

> **Tip:** The rates offered by online banks tend to be higher than the rates offered by traditional ones, because online banks have no retail branches, and therefore less overhead. If you decide to open a savings account with an online bank, investigate it beforehand to see if it has FDIC insurance coverage. To do so, search for the bank's name on the following website:
>
> https://banks.data.fdic.gov/bankfind-suite/bankfind

When deciding whether to invest your funds through a bank, conduct some analysis first. This means calling their customer service phone line to see how easy it is to reach an actual person. If it is not, then consider how difficult it will be to deal with the bank when you actually need it. Second, explore the available options for withdrawing cash. If cash withdrawals are made through an ATM, will your account be charged a fee for doing so? A final investigation is to review the bank's fee structure. How will its charges impact the mix of services that you expect from the bank? If you are investigating multiple banks, then look at these issues for the entire group, and then compare the outcome to determine which one will work best for you.

Another investing option provided by banks is the *certificate of deposit*. This is a term bank deposit with a fixed duration and a stated interest rate. In essence, it is a promissory note issued by a bank. This instrument normally pays a fixed interest rate upon maturity, though some variable-rate versions are available. A more restrictive CD may impose an early-withdrawal penalty (which can be quite large). Given the low interest rate offered for CDs and the restricted nature of early withdrawals, this is generally not a recommended lending arrangement for an investor. If you insist on parking money in a certificate of deposit, then at least shop around first – the differences in interest rates offered can be substantial.

Money Market Funds

A good alternative to a bank is the *money market fund*. These funds are a type of mutual fund that restricts its investments to highly liquid, near-term instruments. They mostly invest in debt securities with high credit ratings and short maturities, such as United States government debt issuances and short-term debt issued by large corporations. Their investment strategy is to offer investors a high level of liquidity, coupled with a very low risk level. In addition, the principal investment in a money market fund does not change in value.

> **Tip:** Most money market fund managers invest in approximately the same securities, so the returns generated by the funds will be about the same. Therefore, to improve your return on investment, select a fund that has a lower operating expense charge.

The convenience offered by money market funds is quite comparable to that of banks, while offering better returns on investment. For example (and depending on the fund), an investor can write checks on her money market fund. Better yet, some of these funds offer tax-free investments, which can be a considerable attraction for those investors in high tax brackets. Other funds offer a debit card, so that you can withdraw cash from the local ATM.

> **Tip:** Use a money market fund to park cash that you plan to repurpose in the near future. For example, if you plan to use dollar cost averaging[5] to slowly invest an inheritance in the stock market, then this is a good place to safely invest the money in the meantime. Or, if you want to maintain a cash reserve for emergencies, this is a good place to keep the money.

> **Tip:** If you are in a high tax bracket, it can make sense to invest in a tax-free money market account. Otherwise, your already-low dividends will receive a tax haircut that results in negligible returns. This is less of an issue if you are investing from within a tax-shielded retirement account.

There is a downside to money market funds, which is that they are not insured by the federal government. However, this is not a major concern, since it is quite difficult for fund investments to decline. In the rare cases where a decline in fund value occurred, the amount of the decline was in the low single digits.

Bonds

A bond is a fixed obligation to pay that is issued by a corporation or government entity to investors. Bonds usually include a periodic interest payment, and are paid off as of a specific maturity date. The interest rates paid on bonds are higher than banks offer for saving accounts and certificates of deposit, and also exceed the rates on money market funds.

The main downside to investing in bonds is that the issuer could go bankrupt. If so, your invested funds may be lost. However, as long as you only invest in highly-rated bonds, the probability of issuer default is quite low. This issue can also be mitigated by investing in a bond fund rather than in individual bonds, so that your investment is spread across many bond issuers.

Another risk associated with bonds is that their resale value can decline as interest rates rise. This is because newer bonds must be offered at higher interest rates, which reduces the demand for your bonds that were issued at lower interest rates. The result is that, if you need to sell a bond before its maturity date, the amount you can obtain for it will be less than its face amount. However, this issue is not a concern if you intend to hold the bond until its maturity date, since it can then be redeemed for its full face amount.

Given the considerations just noted, you should only invest in bonds under certain circumstances. One possibility is when you want to earn a specific amount of income for an extended period of time, since issuers pay out specific amounts of cash at fixed intervals for interest payments. Another possibility is when you need to park the

---

[5] The process of investing the same amount of money in a target security at regular intervals over a certain period of time, regardless of price.

money for a fairly extended period of time, after which it will be spent. For example, if you need to replace production equipment in five years for $100,000, then invest the money in bonds now, in expectation of using the funds in five years. Yet another scenario is to diversify away from your stock investments; this is because bonds tend to appreciate in value when the stock market declines.

Types of Bonds

There are many types of bonds. The list below contains several of the more common ones:

- *Convertible bond.* A convertible bond can be converted into the common stock of the issuer at a predetermined conversion ratio. This can yield a significant gain for the investor if the common stock price of the issuer increases substantially. However, these bonds pay a reduced interest rate, which investors are willing to accept on the grounds that the conversion feature has some value.
- *Deferred interest bond.* A deferred interest bond offers little or no interest at the start of the bond term, and more interest near the end. This format is useful for businesses that currently have little cash with which to pay interest.
- *Income bond.* With an income bond, the issuer is only obligated to make interest payments to bond holders if the issuer or a specific project earns a profit. If the bond terms allow for cumulative interest, then the unpaid interest will accumulate until such time as there is sufficient income to pay the amounts owed.
- *Serial bond.* A serial bond is gradually paid off in each successive year, so the total amount of debt outstanding is gradually reduced.
- *Variable rate bond.* The interest rate paid on a variable rate bond varies with a baseline indicator, which is usually a well-known interest rate.
- *Zero coupon bond.* No interest is paid on a zero coupon bond. Instead, investors buy this bond at a large discount to its face value in order to earn a return on it when it is eventually redeemed. The value of these bonds can drop rapidly if the Fed raises interest rates, so only people with a strong tolerance for risk should purchase them.

Bond Features

Additional features can be added to a bond to make it easier to sell to investors at a higher price. These features are noted below:

- *Sinking fund.* The issuer creates a sinking fund to which cash is periodically added, and which is used to ensure that bonds are eventually redeemed. This feature reduces default risk.
- *Conversion feature.* Bond holders have the option to convert their bonds into the stock of the issuer at a predetermined conversion ratio. This feature increases the potential return for the investor.

- *Guarantees*. The repayment of a bond may be guaranteed by a third party. This feature reduces default risk.

The following additional bond features favor the issuer, and so may reduce the price at which investors are willing to purchase bonds:

- *Call feature*. The issuer has the right to buy back bonds earlier than the stated maturity date.
- *Subordination*. Bond holders are positioned after more senior debt holders to be paid back from issuer assets in the event of a default.

Bond Investment Considerations

There are several issues to consider when making a bond selection. First, if you want to ensure that the price of the bond will remain relatively steady, then buy bonds that mature within the next few years. Since the term to maturity is quite short, changes in the market interest rate will have only a minor impact on the price at which these bonds can be sold in the interim. Conversely, if you plan to hold a bond to maturity, then the number of years remaining is less of a consideration, since you will be obtaining its full face value when it is redeemed by the issuer. If you have no qualms about investing in bonds over the long term, then review the related yield curve (see next) to see if issuers are currently paying a higher interest rate on long-term bonds (which is usually the case). If not, it makes more sense to invest in shorter-term bonds with higher interest rates.

Another investing consideration is how likely a bond issuer is to default. This risk is reviewed by a credit rating agency, which assigns credit ratings to either the issuers of certain kinds of debt, or directly to their debt instruments. There are three major credit rating agencies that provide ratings for the bulk of all debt issuances. They are authorized for ratings work as Nationally Recognized Statistical Rating Organizations (NRSROs) by the SEC. The three agencies that collectively control most of the market are:

- Moody's Investor Service
- Standard & Poor's
- Fitch Ratings

The ratings issued by these agencies are used by investors to determine the price at which to buy bonds. It is difficult to issue bonds without a credit rating, since the issuance might otherwise be undersubscribed or can only be sold at a high interest rate.

The rating classifications used by the agencies vary from each other to some extent. The following table presents a comparison of the credit rating classifications of the three largest agencies. Bond issuances rated as investment grade in the table are considered suitable for investment purposes. The ratings classified as speculative are generally avoided by anyone looking for safe investments.

Credit Rating Comparison

Risk Level	Moody's	Standard & Poor's	Fitch
Investment grade:			
(highest investment grade)	Aaa	AAA	AAA
	Aa1	AA+	AA+
	Aa2	AA	AA
	Aa3	AA-	AA-
	A1	A+	A+
	A2	A	A
	A3	A-	A-
	Baa1	BBB+	BBB+
	Baa2	BBB	BBB
(lowest investment grade)	Baa3	BBB-	BBB-
Speculative grade:			
(highest speculative grade)	Ba1	BB+	BB+
	Ba2	BB	BB
	Ba3	BB-	BB-
	B1	B+	B+
	B2	B	B
	B3	B-	B-
	Caa1	CCC+	CCC+

Note: There are additional lower speculative grades than those listed in this table.

Only a large company with a stable business model and conservative financial practices can hope to qualify for one of the top-tier investment grades. Indeed, so few AAA ratings are issued that the recipients tend to use them as marketing tools to impress customers, suppliers, and employees. Since the AAA rating is well out of reach for most companies, the primary goal is simply to obtain a mid-level investment grade rating. By doing so, investors will not demand an excessively high interest rate on bond issuances. Companies certainly do not want their bonds to be classified as speculative, since investors will not buy them unless the company is willing to pay a very high interest rate.

An issuer may find that the credit rating agencies assign different credit ratings to different bond issuances, even though the bonds are all being issued by the same entity. This variation is caused by differences in the amount of collateral (if any) assigned to the debt, the level of subordination to other debt instruments of the issuer, and other debt terms.

The Yield Curve

A *yield curve* is a graphical representation of the yields on a bond, based on its maturity date. A normal yield curve shows a gradual increase in yield for bonds that mature further in the future, since it is riskier to hold the bonds for a longer period of time. An inverted yield curve presents a declining yield for bonds with longer maturities, which is typically triggered by an expectation that a recession will occur in the future. A flat yield curve is most likely during economic transition periods, when investors are uncertain about whether rates will rise or fall.

Tip: Do not invest in long-term bonds when there is an inverted yield curve, since this condition will likely change within a short period of time, resulting in a drop in the market value of your bonds.

Economists typically review the difference between the interest rate on the 10-year Treasury note and the federal funds rate, which is known as the interest rate spread. For example, if the federal funds rate is 1.50 percent and the 10-year Treasury note rate is yielding 3.25 percent, then the interest rate spread is 1.75 percent, or 175 basis points. This spread embodies the expectations of fixed-income traders about the economy, since their trading activity is setting the yield on the 10-year Treasury note.

When there is a steep yield curve (a large interest rate spread), this is a significant indicator of economic weakness. It typically arises when the Federal Reserve tries to counter a period of economic weakness by lowering its overnight rate, which lowers borrowing costs and therefore encourages lending, which in turn is presumably used to make purchases and fire up the economy. The problem is that the low overnight rate triggers inflationary concerns among fixed-income traders, since inflation lowers the value of principal and interest payments to be received in the future from bonds. Given this concern, the traders sell off their longer-term bond holdings, which are at most risk of a reduction in value from inflation, which lowers their prices and raises their yields. The net effect of these actions is that there is a greater interest rate spread, with a lower short-term rate and a higher yield on longer-term instruments – which represents a steeper yield curve.

The reverse situation can also arise. The Fed may choose to raise interest rates in order to cool off a hot economy, since the higher rate restricts borrowing and therefore dampens purchases. This reduces the risk of long-term inflation, so fixed-income traders are more likely to buy longer-term bonds, thereby raising their prices and lowering their yields. The end result is a flatter yield curve, since the short-term interest rate is rising, while the long-term rate is falling. When this reversal is accelerated, the yield curve can become inverted, where short-term rates are higher than long-term rates. An inverted yield curve is a reasonable predictor of a recession, since the fixed-income traders are expecting a weak economy in the future, which encourages their expectations of low interest rates over the longer-term. The inverted yield curve is not a perfect predictor of a recession, since it has predicted several recessions that did not occur.

U.S. Government Debt Instruments

Despite the continuing increases in the debt of the United States government, its debt instruments are still considered among the lowest-risk in the world. The ones most commonly used by corporations for investment are Treasury Bills (T-Bills) and Treasury Notes (T-Notes). T-Bills have 3, 6, and 12-month maturities. T-Bills having maturities of 3 and 6 months are auctioned on a weekly basis, while T-Bills with 12-month maturities are auctioned once a month. T-Bills are sold at a discount, and redeemed upon maturity at their face value. There is a very active secondary market in T-Bills, so it is easy to sell them prior to their maturity dates.

The maturities of T-Notes range from 1 to 10 years. Two-year T-Notes are issued on a monthly basis, while T-Notes with other maturities are issued on a quarterly basis. T-Notes are available as both inflation-indexed and fixed-rate investments. Interest on T-Notes is paid semi-annually. T-Notes are traded on secondary markets at premiums or discounts to their face values, to reflect the current market interest rate.

Treasury Bonds are also available. Bonds have similar characteristics to T-Notes, but have longer maturities. Maturities are generally in the range of 10 to 30 years.

The government also offers Treasury Inflation-Protected Security (TIPS), which is a Treasury bond that is indexed to an inflationary gauge; doing so protects investors from the decline in the purchasing power of their money. The principal value of TIPS rises as inflation increases, while the interest payment varies with the adjusted principal value of the bond. However, because of the value of this inflation protection feature, the TIPS interest rate is relatively low.

Paradoxically, the trouble with U.S. government debt instruments is their safety – the United States government can obtain the lowest possible interest rates, so there is little return on funds invested in these instruments.

State and Local Government Debt

An interesting investment option is the debt obligations issued by state and local governments. These debt instruments are usually issued in conjunction with the revenue streams associated with large capital projects, such as airport fees and tolls from toll roads. Other instruments are based on general tax revenues. The maturities of these obligations are typically multi-year, so an investor in need of cash must rely upon a vigorous aftermarket to liquidate them prior to their maturity dates. The returns on state and local debt obligations are higher than the yields on federal government issuances, and income from these investments is usually exempt from federal and state taxation. This exemption feature means that these obligations are of great interest to those investors in high tax brackets.

Though it is rare for a state or local government to default on its debt, such cases are not unknown, so be mindful of the reliability of the cash flows supporting debt repayment.

Corporate Bonds

Many larger corporations issue bonds. The interest paid on these bonds is taxable, so a good way to invest in them is from within a retirement account. By doing so, the taxes on any interest income will be deferred. Alternatively, investors in lower tax brackets may invest in corporate bonds without the protection of a retirement account, since the resulting taxes will be relatively low.

How to Buy Bonds

Bonds can be purchased either individually or through a bond fund that contains a selection of bonds. It is generally better to invest in a bond fund, for several reasons. First, the managers of a bond fund will diversify its holdings for you, which is more difficult to do when you are purchasing individual bonds. This diversification covers not just types of bonds, but also their maturities – a bond fund will invest in bonds with a range of maturity dates. Second, the cost to acquire individual bonds is high, sometimes reaching two percent on small purchases. This cost can be hidden, where some brokers include the commission in the price of the bond. Alternatively, the fee charged by a bond fund is usually in the vicinity of ½% per year, which is much more cost-effective. And finally, deciding which bonds to purchase requires a lot of research time to determine the financial viability of the issuer; it is easier to shift this task onto fund managers.

When researching which bonds to buy, a standard set of information will be provided. Explanations for several of these items are noted in the following table, alongside the actual information posted for a bond issued by Xcel Energy, which is a regional electricity provider.

Explanations of Bond Terms

	Terms	Explanation
Issuer	Xcel Energy, Inc.	The name of the bond issuer
Ratings	BB+/Baa1/BBB+	These are the credit ratings issued for the bonds by the various credit rating agencies
Amount	$500 million	The total amount of the bond issuance
Coupon	1.75%	The interest rate that the issuer will pay on the bonds; it is a percent of the maturity value of the bonds
Price	99.777	The current market price of the bonds; it is calculated as the coupon rate divided by the current price
Yield	1.794%	The effective interest rate earned; this is higher than the coupon rate, since the purchase price of the bonds is lower than the face amount
Spread	T+62	The difference between the yield on this bond and the yield on a Treasury bond, expressed as the number of basis points difference
Maturity	March 15, 2027	The date on which the bonds mature

If you want to keep the risk level to a minimum, a good choice is United States Treasury bonds, which are considered to have essentially no risk of default. Of course, the downside of acquiring an investment with no risk is that the return on investment is quite low. Nonetheless, there is a huge market for these bonds. While it is possible to purchase Treasury bonds directly from the United States Treasury (through its treasurydirect.gov website), there are advantages to buying these bonds through your brokerage account. By doing so, you can more easily see the full range of your investments in one place. Also, it is easier to sell Treasury bonds through the broker.

If you choose not to invest through a bond fund or to buy Treasury bonds, then the risk of making a purchase that you will regret increases dramatically. However, there are several best practices to consider that can reduce this risk. Consider the following:

- *Avoid salespeople*. When a brokerage salesperson calls you with a bond buying recommendation, hang up at once. These people are typically on 100% commission compensation plans, so they will push anything in order to make a living. It is much better to do your own research and then buy bonds through a broker that does not employ these salespeople.
- *Buy quality*. Always buy bonds from issuers in excellent financial condition. These issuers also pay rock-bottom interest rates on their bonds, but at least they (almost) never go bankrupt. You can certainly take a chance on a high-yield bond issued by firms in difficult financial condition – but don't be surprised when they default.
- *Diversify holdings*. Economic conditions may impact one industry harder than another, so invest in a range of bonds from issuers located in different industries. Generally, try to cap your bond investment at no more than 5% of the total amount invested in one bond. This means that you should be invested in at least 20 bonds from different issuers. Given this level of diversification, it is easier to just invest in a bond fund.
- *Look for a call feature*. If a bond has a call feature, the issuer can redeem it prior to its maturity date. This is a concern when the interest rate on the bond is a good one, since you may only be able to enjoy the related coupon payments for a short period of time. Generally, try to invest in bonds that have no call feature, or for which the call feature is not activated until a number of years have passed.

Summary

The main problem with lending arrangements is that the interest rate paid is relatively low, especially in comparison to the returns you can receive from stock investments. To enhance the return on these arrangements, use bond funds that have low operating expenses. Their managers will diversify their bond holdings for you, and the low expenses will not cut too deeply into your returns. In addition, try to invest in bonds from within a retirement account, so that the taxes on any income are deferred. These steps can maximize your returns while keeping the associated default risk down to a manageable level.

Chapter 7
Investing in Funds

Introduction

Enormous sums have been invested in both mutual funds and exchange-traded funds, and for good reason. They are an efficient way to invest, are relatively inexpensive, and represent an easy way to diversify your holdings. In this chapter, we compare these fund types, discuss best practices for fund investing, and delve into several related topics.

Mutual Funds vs. Exchange-Traded Funds

The two main types of funds are mutual funds and exchange-traded funds (ETFs). It can be useful to understand what they are, and the differences between them.

A mutual fund is a type of financial vehicle that allows you to pool your money with funds provided by other investors to purchase a collection of stocks, bonds, or other securities. Mutual funds tend to concentrate in either stocks, bonds, or the money market. This collection of investments is known as a portfolio. The price of a mutual fund, which is also known as its net asset value, is calculated as the total value of the securities in the portfolio, divided by the number of the fund's outstanding shares. This price varies constantly, as both the values of the securities and the number of shares outstanding changes.

> **Note:** Mutual fund investors do not actually own the securities in which a fund invests; they only own shares in the fund itself.

If a mutual fund is actively managed, buy and sell decisions are made by its managers and researchers. Their performance benchmark is usually to outperform a well-known index, such as the Standard & Poor's 500 – ideally over a multi-year timeline.

When selecting a mutual fund, the quality of its managers is a consideration. They should come from the top business schools, be certified as Chartered Financial Analysts, and have years of experience in the industry. A high-quality team has deep experience in selected industries, pores over financial statements, meets with company managers to discuss their strategies, and generally has a better understanding of where stocks are undervalued or overvalued.

An essential advantage of using a mutual fund is its level of diversification. The typical fund invests in anywhere from several dozen to over a hundred securities, all spread across different sectors. This level of diversification allows them the opportunity to achieve excellent returns at relatively low risk.

Another advantage of using a mutual fund is the ease with which trades can be conducted. It is usually possible to invest in a fund online, and to issue a withdrawal notification in the same way. Also, if the fund is a money market fund, it may provide check-writing privileges, which means that your access to invested funds is quite similar to what you would have through the local bank – though usually while earning a somewhat higher return on your invested funds.

An exchange-traded fund is a basket of securities that can be bought or sold through a brokerage. ETFs have been constructed for every conceivable asset class, including bonds, gold, and high technology stocks. ETFs are also offered that can enhance your investment leverage, engage in short markets, and avoid short-term capital gains taxes.

An ETF is bought and sold in the same manner as company stock, which means that it has a ticker symbol and price data that can be viewed throughout the trading day. However, unlike company stock, the number of ETF shares outstanding will change every day, due to the continual creation of new shares and redemption of existing ones.

Examples of the types of ETFs currently available are as follows:

- *Bond ETFs*. These funds invest in all types of bonds, including corporate bonds, international bonds, municipal bonds, and U.S. Treasury bonds.
- *Commodity ETFs*. These funds track the price of a commodity, such as gold or corn.
- *Foreign market ETFs*. These funds track markets outside of the United States.
- *Industry ETFs*. These funds invest in specific industries, such as high technology or pharmaceuticals.
- *Market ETFs*. These funds track a specific index, such as the Standard & Poor's 500.
- *Style ETFs*. These funds track an investment style or have a market capitalization focus, such as only investing in small-cap growth stocks.

In addition, a few ETFs are actively managed, which means that they are intended to outperform an index, rather than merely tracking its results.

There are multiple advantages to ETFs. First, they are easy to trade. They can be bought and sold throughout the trading day, while mutual funds only trade at the end of the day. Also, the holdings of an ETF are very transparent, since they are required to publish their holdings every day. Further, ETFs tend to generate fewer capital gain distributions than actively-managed mutual funds. Yet another advantage is their low cost. The operating costs of both ETFs and mutual funds are relatively low and are spread across thousands of investors, so their fees are low. In particular, the trading costs of these funds are much lower than any individual investor can obtain.

There are also some disadvantages to ETFs. First, if an ETF is not frequently traded, there can be a wide bid-ask spread, where investors buy at the high price of the spread and sell at the low price of the spread. Also, ETF sales are not settled for two business days following the sale transaction, which means that the resulting funds are not available for reinvestment for two days.

Both mutual funds and ETFs are extremely safe investments. This is because they maintain a dollar's worth of securities for every dollar invested. Therefore, if you want to withdraw your money from one of these funds, you will receive the current market value of that investment. If the market value of the securities acquired by the fund has declined, then you may receive somewhat less than you invested – but you will not lose your entire investment.

How Exchange-Traded Funds Minimize Taxes

An exchange-traded fund can be an effective vehicle for minimizing or deferring taxes due to its unique structure and trading mechanics. One of the primary tax advantages of ETFs arises from the "in-kind redemption" process. When investors sell shares of an ETF, they typically do so on the open market, which does not trigger a taxable event for the fund itself. If large institutional investors redeem ETF shares, the fund can deliver a basket of underlying securities rather than selling them for cash. This allows the ETF to offload appreciated securities without realizing capital gains, thereby avoiding taxable distributions.

Another tax advantage is that ETFs typically realize fewer capital gains compared to actively managed mutual funds. Because ETFs track indexes and have lower portfolio turnover, they are less likely to sell securities that generate taxable gains. This means investors in ETFs often do not face annual capital gains distributions, allowing gains to compound tax-deferred until the ETF shares are sold.

Additionally, investors can use ETFs to strategically harvest tax losses. By selling a losing ETF and replacing it with a similar fund that tracks a different but correlated index, investors can realize a capital loss without significantly altering their market exposure.

However, it is important to note that these strategies primarily *defer* taxes rather than eliminate them. When you eventually sell your ETF shares, you will owe capital gains tax based on the difference between the sale price and their cost basis. Even so, deferring taxes for years, while enjoying compounding growth, can result in significant after-tax advantages.

Fund Investment Best Practices

While funds are generally a good vehicle for investing your money, there are various best practices available that will increase your odds of generating a greater return on investment, as well as of avoiding losses. These best practices are noted in the following sub-sections.

Reduce Fund Costs

Your rate of return will be deeply impacted by the operating expenses charged by a fund. Even small differences in these charges can build up to major differences in investment returns over time. Therefore, comparison shop among funds to see which ones have a combination of good management and low fees. Typically, a bond fund should charge less than ½% per year, while a stock fund should charge less than 1%. There are several costs to monitor, as noted in the following bullet points:

- It is essential to minimize the *sales load*, which is the commission charged to an investor when buying shares in a mutual fund. If a sales load is charged, then look for alternative funds in which to invest. No-load funds do not have a commission expense associated with them. It is useful to remember that this commission goes to the broker selling you on the fund, not the fund managers. Therefore, it is irrational to assume that a load fund will generate a better return on investment than a no-load fund. In fact, given the added expense of a load fund, its subsequent return on investment will probably be lower than you would have experienced with a no-load fund. In addition, given the presence of a commission, the broker has a strong incentive to push you to invest in a load fund, even when your financial situation clearly indicates that an alternative strategy is warranted.
- Avoid a *back-end load*, which is a fee paid when selling mutual fund shares. It can be a flat fee or gradually decrease over time, usually within five to 10 years. The fund managers make money by using the gradual reduction in the back-end load to convince investors to stay in the fund for a long time, while they charge high annual fees. Once again, this is a commission, which is an unnecessary expense.
- *Minimize operating expenses.* All funds accumulate operating expenses, which are charged through to investors as a deduction from the share price. Over the long term, differences in the expenses charged can have a very noticeable impact on your return on investment. Therefore, it makes sense to favor funds with lower operating expenses. These expenses include trading costs; an actively-managed fund trades frequently, and so will have higher trading costs than a fund that uses a more passive investment strategy. Trading costs tend to be higher when a fund specializes in emerging markets, where the trading environment is smaller and less liquid.
- *Try index funds.* Index funds require minimal management, since they merely invest in an index (such as the S&P 500), seeking to match the performance of that index. No expenses are incurred to engage in research activities. This means that its operating expenses should be extremely low, which benefits the investor.

Note: Index funds are capitalization weighted, which means that the stocks in the fund are held in proportion to their market values within the associated index. If some stocks within an index have inflated valuations, then the associated index fund is forced to invest in a higher proportion of those stocks. If you are uncomfortable with this situation, then invest in an index fund that gives equal weight to all the stocks in the associated index.

Look for Consistent Returns

Some fund managers can generate extraordinary returns for a short period of time, usually by allocating funds toward riskier investments. However, they are more likely to generate significant losses over the longer term, as these investments occasionally perform quite poorly. The result is a high degree of variability in their returns, especially when the market as a whole declines. A better approach is to look for consistent returns within a less risky portfolio of investments. There will still be historical variability in the returns, but not to such an excessive degree.

Avoid Taxes

Invest in funds that do not buy and sell securities very frequently, such as index funds. These funds hold onto investments for long periods of time, resulting in few short-term gains that would be taxed at a higher rate than long-term capital gains.

Allocate Assets

A prudent strategy is to decide upon – and hold to – the percentage of your funds that will be placed in an investment category. For example, you might invest 30% in bond funds, 50% in mutual funds, and 20% in real estate. This allocation is mostly based on your age. When you are younger and so have lots of years in which to weather the vagaries of the stock market, it makes sense to allocate a larger proportion of your assets to the stock market. As retirement approaches, you will probably want to experience more certainty in your returns, so a higher percentage of assets is shifted into bonds. Within each of these allocations, further diversify into different investments. For example, a 50% investment in stocks might then be divvied up into funds that specialize in large-cap stocks, international stocks, and a stock index. By spreading your money among several funds that employ different investing strategies, you can gain from the expertise of fund managers that specialize in different aspects of the market.

Avoid Leveraged Funds

A leveraged fund uses financial derivatives and debt to amplify the return of an underlying index. This strategy can cause problems, because it can lead to significant gains, but also equally large losses. Given the volatility of these funds, they should be avoided.

Invest in Experience

Fund managers with significant experience in the field tend to perform better than those that do not. This is not an overriding factor in selecting a fund, but it can make sense to compare the experience levels of the teams assigned to the management of various funds.

Stock Fund Fundamentals

When investing in stock funds, there are several issues to be aware of. First, only select a fund that invests in a sufficiently large number of stocks. If a fund manager is only invested in 10 stocks, then a catastrophic decline in just one of them will have a major negative impact on the fund's returns. Conversely, if the manager had spread invested funds among 100 stocks, then a few major declines will have little impact.

Another issue to be aware of is how you make money through a stock fund. One way is through the dividends received from the issuers of the stocks held by the fund. The fund manager passes these dividends through to you, or gives you the option to reinvest them in the fund. Unless you need the money, it is better to keep reinvesting the cash, thereby growing your investment stake in the fund. Another way to make money is from capital gain distributions from the fund, which occur when the fund sells stocks for more than their purchase price. As was the case with dividends, you can opt to reinvest these gains in the fund. And finally, the price per share of the fund can increase if the value of its stock holdings increases. This price per share is only a paper profit until such time as you choose to sell the shares. When aggregated, these three sources comprise your total return on investment.

Fund managers invest in accordance with the operating guidelines of the fund, which state its criteria for investment. For example, the guidelines for one fund might state that it only invests in overseas large-cap stocks, while the guidelines for another fund mandate that it invest in small-cap growth stocks. When selecting funds, be sure to peruse their posted summaries of investment guidelines, to better understand what you will be investing in.

> **Note:** Large-cap stocks refer to companies with market capitalizations exceeding $10 billion. Medium-cap stocks refer to companies with market capitalizations between $2 billion and $10 billion, while small-cap stocks refer to companies with market capitalizations between $300 million and $2 billion. Micro-cap stocks refer to companies with market capitalizations below $300 million.

There are different types of investment strategies that a stock fund manager can pursue. For example, an income fund primarily targets stocks that pay out high dividends, while growth funds invest in smaller-cap businesses that are growing rapidly (and which may not be paying dividends at all). Other funds, known as growth and income funds, strike a balance between these extremes, seeking to maximize both stock price growth and dividends. It makes sense to invest in several funds that are targeted at different investment strategies. This might mean that you are investing in both a small-cap growth fund and a large-cap income fund. By doing so, you are spreading your bets across several fund managers and investment strategies.

When investing in international funds, an area of concern is whether a fund is investing in an excessively narrowly-defined region. It is generally not a good idea to invest in a fund that is concentrated within one country, because an economic downturn within a smaller country can have a heavy impact on all stocks associated with that area. A better choice is to invest in an international fund that is broader in scope, perhaps one that invests everywhere outside the United States, or which focuses on a specific region, such as all of South America or Africa. A further issue to be aware of with international stock funds is the impact of changes in the value of various currencies in relation to the U.S. dollar. Generally, a declining dollar valuation increases the value of international stock funds, while a rising dollar decreases their value. International funds can hedge against these valuation changes, but hedges cost money, which increases the operating costs of the fund.

Bond Fund Fundamentals

When investing in bond funds, there are several issues to be aware of. As was the case with stock funds, only select a fund that invests in a sufficiently large number of bonds. Otherwise, a default by one issuer can have an inordinate impact on the returns from a bond fund.

The prices of bond funds tend to be relatively stable when they only invest in short-term bonds. Funds that invest in longer-term bonds are more subject to fluctuations in interest rates. This means that short-term bond funds are a good investment when you want to park some money for a short period of time without having to worry about it declining in value in the interim. In addition, these funds generate a somewhat higher rate of return than money market funds. For example, if you are building up a cash reserve to be used as the down payment on a house a few years from now, a good place to park the money is in a short-term bond fund.

A key aspect of the prices of bond funds is that they move in opposition to interest rates. For example, if interest rates fall, this increases the prices of pre-existing bonds, since they were issued with higher interest rates than the current market rate. Conversely, when interest rates increase, the prices of pre-existing bonds fall, because they now return a lower rate than the current market rate. This means that the prices of bond funds rise and fall in accordance with where market interest rates are at the moment. This also means that you should not buy into a bond fund just because it has a recent history of good performance – that may have more to do with interest rates than the performance of the fund's manager.

> **Tip:** A good way to review the performance of a bond fund is to compare its results to the performance of similar funds with the same investment guidelines. When conducting this comparison, use the *SEC yield* calculation, which approximates the yield an investor would receive in a year by assuming that bonds in the portfolio are held to maturity, all income reinvested, and all fees and expenses factored in.

When comparing the yields advertised by bond funds, be aware that funds play tricks with the yield formulation to make their results look better than those of the competition. First, they may waive some or all of their operating expense charges for a period of time, which amps up their reported yield. This is an especially common trick among new funds that are trying to gain traction in the marketplace. Another trick is to invest a portion of its cash in riskier bonds that have a slightly higher rate of return. These investments may be borderline outside of the stated investment guidelines of the fund.

A third trick is to increase the maturities of the bonds in which it invests, which results in a slightly higher interest rate. When a fund engages in several of these practices at once, it can appear to produce significantly better results than competing funds, allowing it to attract more investor funds.

An especially good reason to avoid load funds is that, given the extra fees charged, their managers are under extra pressure to provide good performance to investors. This pressure can lead them to invest aggressively, such as by investing in lower-quality bonds in the expectation that the economy will improve, which will raise the value of these bonds. If these fund managers are incorrect in their assumptions, then their funds are at increased risk of producing poor results. In short, more costly funds can actually return worse results than lower-cost funds whose managers simply buy and hold bonds for the long term.

Bond Fund Selection Process

There are several steps to go through when deciding upon the right bond fund for you. The first step is to keep your costs down, thereby enhancing your long-term returns. This means selecting a fund that has low operating costs – of which there are not many. Fee structures tend to be high, so eliminating high-cost funds from consideration will likely eliminate 90% of the available funds.

The second step in the selection process is to determine the length to maturity that you want, and then review the investment guidelines of the remaining funds to determine which ones meet your criteria. For example, a short-term bond fund invests in bonds with maturities of less than five years, while an intermediate-term fund invests in bonds with maturity dates that are between two and 10 years, and a long-term fund invests in bonds with maturity dates of ten years or more. The yields generated from a short-term bond fund are the lowest, while those from a long-term fund are the highest. Investing in intermediate-term and long-term funds makes the most sense when you intend to invest your funds for a long period of time, and are willing to tolerate more volatility in the value of the bond fund. The values of long-term bond funds are the most volatile, so only invest here if you are comfortable with a higher degree of uncertainty.

Once you have found a set of lower-cost bond funds that invest in bonds with the right maturities, review the credit ratings of the bonds in which they invest. Bonds with a poor credit rating generate a higher return, while bonds with excellent credit ratings generate a lower return. The choice is up to you, based on how much risk you are willing to tolerate.

Finally, review the taxability of the interest being passed through to you. Taxable interest is fine, as long as you are investing funds from a tax-deferred retirement account. If that is not the case, and especially if you are in a high tax bracket, then tax-free bonds might be a better choice.

In short, there are a number of selection criteria to work through before you can select a bond fund that works best for your specific needs.

Hybrid Funds

A variation on stock funds and bond funds is a fund that invests in both areas, which is called a hybrid fund. These funds are not limited to just stocks and bonds. For example, a hybrid fund might invest in stocks and real estate, or bonds and gold.

A hybrid fund is targeted at achieving greater diversification, thereby reducing investment risk. The level of risk associated with a fund is based on its investing guidelines, which may vary from conservative to aggressive.

There are several variations on the concept. A balanced fund follows a standard asset allocation proportion, such as 60% in stocks and 40% in bonds. A blended fund includes a mix of value and growth stocks. A target date fund begins with a more aggressive allocation, and then gradually rebalances to a more conservative allocation, to be used by a specific date in the future. In the last case, the asset allocation proportion will change over time. In all cases, the fund manager actively manages the individual asset holdings within each asset category to respond to changes in market conditions, as well as to take advantage of possible capital appreciation opportunities.

Summary

We advocate the use of funds, and especially the use of multiple funds, because they allow you to diversify your money among a large number of investments. By doing so, a few failures will be offset by gains elsewhere in your portfolio. A further advantage of funds is that they are professionally managed and (depending on the fund) are relatively inexpensive. This means that you can benefit from expert advice without spending too much for the privilege. In short, investing in funds is an excellent choice.

Chapter 8
Investing in Property

Introduction

A discerning investor can earn substantial returns from real estate. However, significant judgment is required to ensure that a property is of a sufficient quality level, that the price paid for it is reasonable, and that it is operated in a profitable manner. In this chapter, we cover the advantages and disadvantages of investing in real estate, the types of real estate investments, how to acquire them, and several related topics.

Advantages of Investing in Real Estate

There are several good reasons why it makes sense to invest in real estate. Consider the following items:

- *Below-market purchases*. It is sometimes possible to acquire real estate at a below-market price – especially when the seller needs to sell quickly, and you have sufficient cash on hand to fill this need. Taking advantage of these anomalies requires a deep knowledge of local market prices, which is easier to obtain when you commit to real estate investing on a full-time basis.
- *Cash inflows*. When a property is currently being rented out, it generates a stream of monthly rent payments. Some properties may have additional payments associated with them, such as for washers and dryers, storage, and parking. Depending on the offsetting cash outflows for mortgage payments, property taxes, maintenance, and so forth, the net cash inflows may be substantial.
- *Depreciation tax shield*. The depreciation[6] expense that can be claimed on a real estate investment involves no cash outflow, and yet reduces the amount of taxable income – thereby shielding you from a portion of the taxes that would otherwise be due. Currently, the depreciation period for residential real estate is 27½ years, while the depreciation period for commercial buildings is 39 years.
- *Property appreciation*. Depending on the area, real estate tends to appreciate – depending on local demand levels. This can vary substantially within even a short distance, but if you choose property carefully, it can appreciate quite substantially over a long period of time. Also, if you are good at fixing up real estate, doing so may trigger a substantial increase in property value.
- *Leverage effects*. Real estate is usually purchased with the assistance of a substantial mortgage, typically in the range of 70-80% of the purchase price. This means that any returns from the property are magnified by the amount of this debt. For example, if you use a $50,000 down payment to acquire a $300,000

---

[6] Depreciation is the planned, gradual reduction in the recorded value of an asset over its useful life by charging it to expense. Land cannot be depreciated.

rental property and then earn $25,000 per year from it, you have generated a return of 50% on your $50,000 down payment – because so much debt was used to fund the purchase.

- *Tax deferral.* You do not pay income tax on any increases in the value of property until you sell it, which may not take place until years after the initial investment. In addition, it is possible under the current tax laws to roll the gain over into another real estate investment, thereby extending the tax deferral period even further.
- *Rate of increase in income.* If it is possible to increase rental rates at the rate of inflation, then your income gradually increases, since the fixed-rate mortgage being paid off (your primary expense) does *not* increase at the rate of inflation. The following example illustrates the concept.

EXAMPLE

Sarah Henderson buys a single-family home for $300,000 that she plans to rent out. She makes a 20% down payment on the property and takes out a 30-year fixed rate mortgage at 5% for the $240,000 remaining amount of the purchase price. The ongoing monthly cash inflows and outflows associated with the property are as follows:

Mortgage payment	$1,400
Property tax	350
Maintenance, insurance, other costs	550
Monthly rent payment	2,600

Currently, Sarah is receiving $2,600 of rental income and paying out $2,300 for various expenses and debt repayments, for a monthly profit of $300. In the following table, we note the results for Sarah over the subsequent 10 years, assuming that the rent payment and all expenses except the fixed mortgage payment increase at a rate of 2% per year, while the value of the home appreciates at a rate of 3% per year.

Year	Monthly Cash In	Monthly Cash Out	Net Cash Flow	Annual ROI*	Property Value
1	$2,600	$2,300	$300	6.0%	$300,000
2	2,652	2,318	334	6.7%	309,000
3	2,705	2,336	369	7.4%	318,270
4	2,759	2,355	404	8.1%	327,818
5	2,814	2,374	440	8.8%	337,652
6	2,871	2,393	478	9.6%	347,782
7	2,928	2,413	515	10.3%	358,216
8	2,987	2,434	553	11.1%	368,962
9	3,046	2,454	592	11.8%	380,031
10	3,107	2,476	631	12.6%	391,432

ROI = return on investment

The key takeaways from the preceding table are that the net cash flow from the property will gradually increase over time, and that the property value should increase substantially over time. Both of these factors should generate significant wealth for Sarah over the long-term. In particular, the net cash flows from the property increase so much that her return on investment doubles by the end of the 10-year period.

Disadvantages of Investing in Real Estate

Despite the positives noted in the preceding section, there are a few disadvantages to be aware of before investing in real estate – some of them significant enough to keep you from proceeding. They are as follows:

- *Grind it out.* The returns from real estate investing generally only accrue over an extended period of time, and only if you purchase judiciously and invest enough to properly maintain properties. Also, depending on the types of properties acquired and the nature of your tenants, it may be necessary to spend a substantial amount of time managing the properties.
- *Variability of income.* You may lose money in some periods. This is especially likely when only a small down payment was made, resulting in larger mortgage payments. Also, in periods when demand is soft, a property may not be rented at all or it will not be possible to raise the rental rate as much as you would like.
- *Unexpected maintenance.* There may be times when unexpected maintenance issues arise, such as a failed water heater or a leaky roof. The associated repair or replacement costs may be substantial, and could wipe out your cash reserves.
- *Rent control.* If you are investing in residential units, there is a possibility that the local government will impose rent controls, which severely limit your ability to raise rents.
- *Time requirement.* Investing in real estate requires a significant amount of time. You will need to spend time learning about the neighborhoods in which you want to invest, identifying problems with prospective investment opportunities, and dealing with maintenance issues. It is possible to hire a property manager to deal with tenants, but dealing with the property manager will still require a certain amount of time.
- *Transaction costs.* The transaction costs associated with buying and selling properties can be quite steep. These costs, which include commissions, title insurance, loan origination fees, and a variety of closing costs, can easily wipe out the appreciation in market value of a property. These costs can only be offset by holding onto properties for an extended period of time, so that they can appreciate to a substantial degree. A large part of these costs is the real estate agent's commission, which varies by type of property. The following table contains the ranges of commissions that are typically paid out for various types of property sales, with these amounts being split between the agents representing the buyer and seller.

Real Estate Commissions by Property Type

Property Type	Commission Range
Larger investment properties	1-3%
Raw land	10%
Single-family homes and condominiums	5-6%
Smaller multi-family and commercial properties	3-5%

- *Tax payouts.* Ongoing income from real estate, as well as gains from the sale of a property, are all subject to federal and state income taxes – which can be substantial.
- *Valuation declines.* It is entirely possible that the market value of real estate will decline sharply over the short term, especially when it was preceded by a bubble in property values that sent prices surging higher than the long-run trend. If you buy property near its peak price with a modest down payment, experience a valuation decline and then sell at the bottom of the market, it is quite possible that the entire amount of your down payment will be lost.
- *Rent declines.* During economic contractions, it can be difficult to find quality tenants. If the contraction is prolonged, you may be faced with ongoing mortgage, maintenance, and utility payments without any offsetting rental payments.
- *Leverage effects.* The leverage effect already noted as an advantage of investing in real estate can also be a disadvantage, magnifying your losses. To return to the earlier example of using a $50,000 down payment to acquire a $300,000 rental property, what if the result is a $25,000 loss in the first year? You will have generated a return of -50% on your $50,000 down payment, wiping out half of the investment. Thus, using debt to buy properties can very much work in your favor – or against it.
- *Liquidity.* It can be difficult to sell off real estate within a short period of time. This can be a problem if you have an immediate need for a significant amount of cash. When you are really pressed for cash, a vulture investor may swoop in and offer cash immediately at a steep discount to the market price of the property.

These disadvantages can be mitigated by holding real estate for many years, maintaining a cash reserve to keep you solvent during any negative cash flow situations, and rolling your gains from property sales over into new property investments (in order to avoid taxes). In short, there are disadvantages to real estate investing, but there are ways to keep them from overwhelming you.

Types of Real Estate Investments

There are several types of investment opportunities available, each with its own ac-quisition, operating, and tax characteristics that make it more or less attractive to the investor. Their characteristics are noted in the following sub-sections.

Purchase a Residence

The most basic real estate investment is acquiring your own residence. This can be considered an investment, because you will gradually build equity in the property as the mortgage is paid off over time. In addition, people frequently downsize once they retire, buying their retirement property for substantially less than the amount they re-ceived from sale of their prior residence; the difference can be used as retirement funding. In addition, a gain of up to $250,000 (or $500,000 for married couples filing jointly) is not subject to tax. To qualify for this exclusion, the taxpayer must have owned and used the home as a principal residence for at least two of the past five years. An option to take advantage of a reduced exclusion can be obtained by applying to the IRS. The IRS will consider situations in which a taxpayer had to change resi-dences in less than the mandated holding period due to a job change or health reasons. If approved, the reduced exclusion is calculated as the ratio of the period of use during the past five years to two years.

EXAMPLE

A taxpayer is forced to sell his home after one year due to health reasons and move into an assisted living facility. The IRS approves his request for a reduced exclusion. The calculation of the reduced exclusion amount is 50%, which is one year of residence divided by the mini-mum two-year requirement.

Convert a Residence to a Rental

When moving to a new home, it can make sense to retain ownership of the old prop-erty and rent it out. This approach is most viable when you are staying within the local area, and so can more easily oversee the rental property. Another benefit is avoiding the transaction costs associated with selling the property. And yet another advantage is that you already lived in the home, and so are already aware of any maintenance issues it may have. In addition, the unit is now classified as an investment property, so that you can take a depreciation deduction, as well as deductions for all business expenses associated with it. These expenses include the costs to advertise the property rental, insurance, and maintenance costs.

A variation on the concept is to rent out a portion of your home. When this is done, the rent received is treated as taxable income. When you rent property for less than 15 days during the year and use it as a personal residence the rest of the time, you do not have to include the rent in your income; when this is done, you cannot deduct any rental expenses.

Upgrade and Sell Your Home

If you like fixing up homes, an investment option is to buy a home with maintenance issues, put time and money into upgrading it, sell the home, and move on to the next fixer-upper. This approach requires you to focus on upgrades that will increase the value of the home. Also, you must live in the home for at least two years in order to take advantage of the capital gains exemption of up to $250,000 (or $500,000 for married couples filing jointly).

EXAMPLE

Henry buys a fixer-upper home for $240,000 and moves in. Over the next two years, he spends $30,000 on materials, as well as many hours of his personal time, to make a variety of up-grades. Two years later, he sells the home for $360,000. This is a profit of $90,000 over his $270,000 investment, and represents a two-year return of 33%.

This approach is only recommended for those investors who like to deal with ongoing construction activities, find that moving frequently is not a burden, and are good at locating under-valued fixer-uppers. A final concern is that the transaction costs associated with continually buying and selling properties every few years can be substantial, and will offset a large portion of the profits generated.

Buy a Second Home

You may elect to purchase a second home and use it as a vacation home. You could keep the home only for your personal use. If so, the only investment return will be from the eventual sale of the property, based on any appreciation in its value. Offsetting this appreciation return will be the ongoing costs of purchasing and maintaining the home, including mortgage payments, insurance, property taxes, utilities, maintenance, and so forth. In addition, it may be necessary to hire a property management firm to watch the property. Generally, these ongoing expenditures more than offset any gains from property value appreciation, making a vacation home the least profitable of all real estate investments.

As was the case with your primary residence, you may elect to rent out the vacation home. When this is the case, the rent received is treated as taxable income. When you rent property for less than 15 days during the year and use it as a personal residence the rest of the time, you do not have to include the rent in your income; when this is done, you cannot deduct any rental expenses.

A variation is to rent out the vacation home the majority of the time, in which case the tax situation matches that of any other real estate investment. In this case, you are permitted to personally use the property for up to 14 days per year, or less than 10% of the days when the property is rented, and still take advantage of all the tax benefits associated with a rental unit.

The definition of personal use includes not only the days you personally use the property, but also your family members, the days you have donated for use of the property, and any days it was rented out for less than its fair market value. Thus, a donation of a week of time to a local charity auction would be considered personal use. Conversely, any time spent at the home doing maintenance does not count as personal time. Thus, if you spend a month fixing up a vacation home, it does not count as personal time.

Buy a Timeshare

A *timeshare* is a form of fractional ownership, where buyers purchase the right to occupy a unit of real estate over specified periods. For example, purchasing one week of a timeshare means the buyer owns 1/52nd of the unit. Buying one month equates to one-twelfth ownership. This model can be applied to many types of properties, such as vacation resorts, condominiums, and apartments.

There are many problems with timeshares that make them a poor real estate investment. In the following bullet points, we show why there are much better investments than timeshares:

- *Purchase price*. Timeshares are extremely expensive. Because you are only purchasing a fraction of the total time period for a unit, the developer can easily mask the fact that the price being paid is much higher than the market value of the underlying real estate.
- *Maintenance fees*. The maintenance fees charged for a timeshare start off low, when the property is relatively new, and then increase as it ages. These fees can be so high that they exceed the cost of simply renting a room at a nearby hotel for the same period of time.
- *Exchange problems*. It can be difficult to exchange your time slot and location for a different one, and doing so will probably require an extra fee. It may not be possible to secure a desired time slot or location at all, if it is at a busy resort.
- *Cost of debt*. Lenders do not like to lend money for the purchase of a timeshare. Those lenders that do offer mortgages will likely impose a higher-than-average interest rate.
- *Sale difficulty*. It is extremely difficult to sell a timeshare. Thousands of timeshare owners want to stop paying high maintenance fees, which has created an excess amount of timeshare supply, against which there is too little demand. The result is strong downward pressure on the prices at which timeshares can be sold. So many people want to sell their timeshares that there are consulting firms that charge a fee to assist in this process, or to help cancel a timeshare entirely.

Options for getting rid of a timeshare include gifting it to someone else, selling it at a significant loss, or renting out. A common option is to sell off a timeshare at a loss, just to avoid the ongoing maintenance fees.

In short, the only people who make money on timeshares are the developers who built and operate these properties. Investing in them is not advised.

> **Tip:** Avoid purchasing a fractionalized interest in *any* real estate; this is a common ploy by a developer to jack up the total price of a property by spreading the price among many investors.

Buy a Residential Property

There are several types of residential properties worth investing in. In the following bullet points, we note the key characteristics of each one:

- *Apartment buildings.* A particular advantage of owning an apartment building is that a majority of the units are generally rented out, so that some cash inflow can be expected in every month. On the other hand, there will be multiple tenants (and their problems) to deal with, which requires a relatively high level of oversight, and quite possibly the hiring of a property manager. These buildings tend to appreciate well over time, if they are properly maintained and located in a desirable neighborhood.
- *Single-family homes.* Single-family homes tend to appreciate in value faster than attached homes (such as townhouses), because there is more demand for this type of real estate. The main downside is that renting is an all-or-nothing proposition, where either the entire unit is rented or it stands empty.

> **Tip:** Only buy residential property in places where the cost to rent equals or exceeds the cost to own a home. When the cost to own exceeds the cost to rent, the market prices in the area are inflated.

- *Condominiums.* These are large property complexes that are comprised of individual units, each of which is owned separately. Ownership of one of these units means that you own the interior of a unit, as well as a proportionate interest in all common areas, such as the grounds and hallways. The home-owners' association actually owns and maintains the common areas, as well as the building structure. The maintenance costs tend to be lower for a condominium, since much of the exterior maintenance is handled by the home-owners' association – which benefits from volume purchases. A downside is that condominium demand tends to be lower than for single-family homes, so their market price appreciates at a slower rate.

> **Tip:** Do not invest in condominiums located in older buildings, since they have aging plumbing, ventilation, and electrical systems that are in need of overhauls – and which result in very high assessments from the homeowners' association.

- *Cooperatives.* These are a form of shared housing in which each owner purchases a share of the entire building, which is represented by a stock certificate. The purchase gives you the right to inhabit a specific area within the building. The problem with cooperatives is that the association of homeowners must approve any remodeling plans and rental arrangements, and may even require the prior approval of a buyer. Given the severity of these restrictions, it is rarely a good idea to invest in a cooperative.

Flip a Residential Property

It is generally best to buy and hold residential property, in order to benefit from its appreciation in value over many years. An alternative approach is to buy and flip property. This strategy works best in hot markets where there is not enough available housing to meet demand, resulting in spiraling prices.

There are two ways to make money with the flipping strategy. One approach is to find a motivated seller who is willing to sell at a below-market price, and then immediately sell the property at full retail price. The other option is to buy a run-down property, make a number of judiciously-selected upgrades to maximize its price, and then sell it. In both cases, the intent is to sell the property quickly, in order to tie up capital for the minimum amount of time.

A key risk associated with flipping properties is transaction costs, which include inspection fees, closing costs, commissions, and title insurance. Another risk is that the cost of basic maintenance issues, as well as upgrade costs, turn out to be higher than expected, wiping out your anticipated profits. And yet another problem is the amount of time that a property will sit empty before it can be sold to a new buyer – during which it accrues mortgage interest costs, property taxes, utilities, homeowners' association dues, and so forth. A final concern is that you are not holding the property for very long, and so will pay ordinary income tax on any profit earned. In short, flipping properties is a risky strategy – despite the number of shows about this practice on television.

A further concern is that real estate prices might drop while you own the property, so that its eventual sale is at a reduced price that might result in a loss. This scenario is more likely in a hot real estate market where lots of investors are piling in, hoping to flip their investments in short order for a profit. If a large number of these investors sense that the market is turning and sell off their properties, demand can dry up quickly, resulting in a sharp price decline. In this situation, you might be forced to retain ownership of the property for years, renting it out until prices return to a point at which it makes sense to sell.

In short, flipping property might initially sound like a good way to turn a profit within a short period of time, but this activity is impacted by so many risks that earning any reasonable amount of profit is actually quite difficult.

Buy Commercial Property

The commercial property classification is a broad one. It includes hotels, industrial, mobile home parks, offices, retail, self-storage, warehousing, and similar properties. Each of these property types requires significant expertise, so it makes sense to concentrate on one type in a specific area. By doing so, you can gain a better understanding of the quirks of the local market, and when there are pricing anomalies that can be exploited to generate above-average returns.

Investing in commercial property is an especially good idea when you can use some of the acquired space for your own business. By doing, you can avoid paying rent to a third party. In addition, being located on-site makes it easier to keep in touch with the other tenants, and learn about any problems they might be having with the facility.

There are several major concerns to be aware of when delving into commercial property investments. One is the risk that a property could have a high vacancy rate for an extended period of time. This can be caused by speculative construction in the area, as well as downturns in the economy that cool demand for office space. Another issue is that prospective tenants may demand costly upgrades to match their particular needs before they will agree to move in; this can represent a major cash outflow that may not be recovered from ongoing rent payments for several years. Alternatively, a prospective tenant may demand several months of free rent as part of a lease deal; this does not represent a cash outflow, but it does result in the absence of any cash inflows for a period of time. A final concern is that smaller tenants (which are your most likely pool of tenant candidates) are more likely to go out of business, leaving you with empty office space until a replacement can be found.

> **Tip:** Do not invest in commercial real estate when the supply of available space is increasing faster than the rate of demand for that space. This supply-demand imbalance will likely trigger a drop in lease rates.

Buy Undeveloped Land

A final possibility is to acquire undeveloped land. The strategy in doing so is to make the acquisition just before anyone else realizes that the land is about to be developed – perhaps to expand a nearby airport or to house a sports stadium. This is a dangerous approach, since the land does not generate any positive cash flow in the meantime, and you will have to at least pay property taxes on it every year. Furthermore, an investment in land that may not pay off for several years represents an opportunity cost, since the cash used to buy it could have been more profitably employed elsewhere. Also, lenders are less willing to issue mortgages on undeveloped land, since these loans are less likely to be paid off. To reduce their risk, lenders require a higher down payment, and will probably charge a higher interest rate. And to make things even more difficult, land cannot be depreciated, so there is no tax write-off associated with land investments.

The situation is quite different when the intent is to acquire undeveloped land, have it zoned for a particular type of real estate (such as residential housing) and then subdivide it into the authorized type of housing. Some investors sell out to property developers at this point, while others will engage in the construction process – though that requires forming a construction company to conduct the work.

Anyone investing in raw land should be aware of the following issues before doing so, in order to mitigate the risk of loss:

- *Monitor supply and demand.* Only acquire land in areas where there is robust demand for property, and especially when there is a shortage of available land.

71

- *Understand land access.* Have a clear understanding of the access rights to the property you want to acquire. If it is entirely landlocked, it may not be possible to acquire access, in which case the property is useless.
- *Understand the applicable zoning.* The local government will have zoned the property for a certain type of use. If you are contemplating a different type of development, and especially if local sentiments are against what you are proposing, then it is quite unlikely that the zoning will be altered to accommodate your wishes.
- *Understand cash outflows.* Be very clear about the tax, insurance, and other costs that will be incurred before you can sell the property to another party. Then estimate the longest period that you will likely need to hold it, and calculate the total cash outflow that you will incur during this period. Do you have sufficient cash reserves to sustain these losses?
- *Understand development costs.* When the intent is to develop the land to a certain extent before selling it to a developer, have a clear understanding of the costs that you will incur. This may involve expenditures for surveying, permits, and environmental studies – after which there will be payments for running utilities, installing stormwater controls, building roads, and so forth.

How to Acquire Real Estate

It always makes sense to acquire real estate for the lowest possible price, in order to achieve the highest possible gains thereafter. There are several ways to make below-market acquisitions, as we will detail in the following sub-sections.

Foreclosures

A *foreclosure* is the act of taking possession of a mortgaged property when the borrower fails to make scheduled mortgage payments. Once the lender has taken possession, it contracts with a local property management firm to prepare the property for sale. It then sells the property in order to generate enough cash to pay off the mortgage. The property sale is conducted at an auction, for which state laws have varying requirements for general notification – typically a posting in the local newspaper. Consider subscribing to one of the many local services that keep track of these notices, and which will forward them to you via email for a fee.

You can bid for these properties, and may score a below-market purchase. However, a number of large investment funds have also entered the business of buying foreclosed properties, and may outbid you or offer a package deal to the bank, buying a cluster of its foreclosed properties for cash. Another concern is that prospective bidders are rarely allowed to inspect a property prior to the auction, which presents the risk of learning about major problems only after you own it. A further issue is that 10% of the purchase price must usually be paid in cash at the auction, with the remainder due within 30 days; this can be a concern for a cash-strapped investor.

There are several points in the foreclosure process at which it is possible to acquire a property. Your options for profiting from the process vary, depending on which of these steps you choose to participate in. The options are as follows:

1. *Preforeclosure*. The preforeclosure period starts with the first time a home-owner misses a mortgage payment and extends through the notice of default filing by the lender. This is the point at which the borrower first begins to struggle with making payments. At this stage, it may be possible to approach the borrower with a buyout offer; accepting it will keep the borrower from having a foreclosure listed on his or her credit report, which may be tempting enough to allow for a low price being paid. This is an especially good option when you can make an all-cash offer, so that the borrower can walk away from the property in short order with some cash.

2. *Notice of default*. The next phase in the foreclosure process is when the lender files a notice of default. This triggers a multi-month process in which the lender gains the right to sell the property. At this point, the borrower is even more motivated to sell. However, the notice of default is accessible to the public, which means that other investors may possibly approach the buyer about a quick sale – which increases the level of competition, and therefore the price that will probably have to be paid to secure the property. A possible option here is to assume the borrower's mortgage, though this will be subject to the agreement of the lender, which will probably require a loan application and fee payment.

3. *Foreclosure sale*. The next phase in the foreclosure process depends on the state. In a state that requires a judicial foreclosure, the lender must sue the borrower, which results in a court hearing where the court usually rules in favor of the lender, allowing a sale to proceed. The lender then advertises the sale and hires a third party to conduct a public auction. In a state that does *not* require a lawsuit, the lender can proceed to a property sale more quickly. If those cases in which there is no bidder, the lender bids the outstanding amount of its loan, plus any penalties and fees, and takes possession of the property. You should set rules in advance of the bidding process, with a firm cap on how much you are willing to bid. Otherwise, you may end up with a property on which it is impossible to earn a profit. Or, if the lender ends up owning the property, it might be possible to negotiate a purchase immediately after the foreclosure sale, before the lender incurs any additional costs to start market-ing the property for sale.

4. *Redemption period*. Some states permit a borrower to redeem property after a loan default has occurred, but before it has been foreclosed. Under these right of redemption rules, the borrower must pay back all the remaining principal, as well as any interest due and other costs incurred by the lender because of the default event. It may be possible to acquire the borrower's redemption rights, allowing you to make the required redemption payment and take pos-session of the property.

5. *Lender purchase*. In most cases, the lender will end up with title to a fore-closed property. When this happens, responsibility for the property is shifted

to a department within the lender that dispositions these properties. It can make sense to learn about the procedures used by this department to sell off properties, which usually involves having local real estate brokers handle the sales work. The best way to acquire a property from a lender at this stage is to make an offer for a property that the lender would otherwise have to fix up before it can be ready for sale. The lender may be interested, if doing so can clear a nonperforming asset off its balance sheet in short order, and without consuming any more cash.

> **Tip:** Do not begin to upgrade a property acquired at a foreclosure sale until the borrower's redemption period has ended. Otherwise, you will have invested in a property that is now owned by someone else.

Prior to making a bid, you should evaluate all structural problems and other maintenance issues with a property, itemizing the expenditures that will be needed to bring the property up a level at which it can be profitably rented. In addition, research whether there are any outstanding tax liens on the property. Based on this research, determine what your target price will be, and also establish a not-to-exceed bidding threshold. The threshold is mandatory – otherwise, there is a good chance that you will overbid in the heat of a competitive auction, and will then be burdened with an unprofitable investment.

Probate Sales

When a person dies, his or her estate enters a legal process known as probate. The probate process is overseen by a legal system administered by a probate court. When a deceased person owns real estate, it must be sold at the best possible price in order to maximize the value of the estate. The sale of this real estate is overseen by a probate court.

The court's first step is to authorized a real estate agent to list the property for sale. Next, the court sets a listing price, which is usually based on an appraisal and advice from the listing agent. At this point bidders can make an offer, which must be accompanied by a 10% down payment, usually in the form of a cashier's check. The estate representative is required to accept the highest bid, which will be made official after the court accepts the offer. During the court hearing, other bidders are allowed to make offers (called overbids[7]) that exceed the original offer. Also, family members of the decedent must be notified of the sale, and given time to comment on its terms.

A probate sale can be risky for an investor, especially because the rules about these sales vary by state. To ensure that you do not make any mistakes and possibly forfeit a down payment, be sure to work with a real estate agent and a real estate attorney during the process. Also, be sure to obtain a detailed inspection of the property prior to making an offer.

---

[7] Overbids are generally not allowed unless they exceed the current bid by at least five percent.

Despite these issues, many investors favor probate sales. This is because the more complicated sales process tends to drive away some bidders, resulting in less demand and therefore lower purchase prices. In addition, probate sales occur at all times, even during economic downturns when property owners are generally not willing to sell – which can result in lower purchase prices than would normally be obtained. And finally, probate sales can be considered an alternative property distribution channel, through which potentially high-value properties will be sold. In short, there are good reasons to keep tabs on probate sales in your area.

Short Sales

A *short sale* occurs when a homeowner sells his or her property to a third party for less than the amount due on the associated mortgage, with all proceeds going to the lender. This situation can be triggered when there is a decline in the value of real estate, so that borrowers have negative equity in their properties. It can also occur when a borrower has taken out a loan for more than the market value of the associated property, and is then unable to make the required payments. In both cases, if the borrower were to sell at the current market price, they would still owe money to the lender. For example, a homeowner has lost his job and the value of his house has declined, so he cannot make any additional payments on the $200,000 mortgage. Instead, he sells the property for $180,000, leaving a $20,000 deficiency that the lender agrees in advance to waive.

It may be possible for an investor to identify short-sale opportunities by subscribing to a service that tracks all notices of default issued by lenders. The trouble is, once a notice of default becomes public knowledge, other investors may contact the borrower as well, resulting in multiple offers to buy the property. If the borrower is interested in your proposal, the next step is to locate the person within the lender's bureaucracy who is empowered to deal with short sale proposals, which can be a difficult chore. All short sale paperwork should be sent to this person.

Note: The original lender may have sold off its nonperforming mortgages to a third party for a discounted amount. Since the new loan holder paid less to acquire these mortgages, it may be more interested in accepting a short sale proposal – doing so allows it to convert a mortgage into cash, while still earning a profit.

Before the short sale process can begin, the lender must sign off on the decision to execute the sale. As part of this process, it will request documentation that clarifies why a short sale is being requested. The borrower will need to submit a financial package to the lender that proves his or her financial hardship, including financial statements, W-2 forms, payroll stubs, and bank statements. In addition, the listing agent sends the lender the buyer's purchase offer and a copy of the earnest money check. The submission package must be persuasive, since the lender will lose money on the transaction. Also, given the lender's loss, the process tends to be quite slow, and may take many months to complete. It is entirely possible that the lender will not accept the proposal; if it believes more money can be made through a standard fore-closure, then it may elect to take that approach instead.

> **Tip:** Have ready access to 100% of the cash needed to complete a short sale, perhaps through a pre-approved loan. Any lender that is about to take a loss on a short sale will only take cash to close the deal; it will not offer financing.

Despite the bureaucracy involved, borrowers in difficult circumstances may be amenable to a short sale, since this approach has a less negative impact on their credit rating. With a short sale, they can get out from under a mortgage they cannot afford, and no foreclosure appears on their credit report. In addition, they may be able to stay on the premises and rent from the new property owner.

The majority of short-sale properties are listed on the websites of real estate agents. These listings may not clearly identify a property as being a short sale transaction. Instead, look for wording that offers are subject to bank approval.

> **Note:** There is no borrower redemption requirement in a short sale, so investors do not have to worry about having the prior owner take back a property.

Installment Sales

Usually, the buyer of a property pays the seller in full, either directly in cash or with a mortgage obtained from a third party. Sometimes, however, the seller provides the buyer with financing, in which case the buyer makes a series of payments to the seller over a period of time. If this arrangement qualifies as an installment sale, then the seller can incrementally report gains from the sale upon the receipt of each individual payment. This arrangement is allowed by the tax code so that sellers providing financing do not have to report the entire amount of a gain at the point of sale without having actually received payment in full from the buyer. A further benefit for the seller is that a series of partial gains recognized over multiple tax years may put the seller in a lower tax bracket, resulting in a lower overall tax. However, a seller may elect out of an installment sale arrangement when it wants to recognize the entire amount of a gain at the point of sale, perhaps because there is a loss to offset, or tax rates are expected to rise in the future.

A sales arrangement qualifies as an installment sale when at least one payment will be received in a later tax year. However, installment sales treatment is not allowed when a loss will result from the sale of property; in this case, the full amount of the loss must be reported in the year of sale.

When receiving payments under an installment sales arrangement, the seller reports as income that portion of the payments received that comprise a gain from the sale, as well as the interest income associated with the loan extended to the buyer. The amount of gain is reported ratably as each payment is received from the buyer. The gain reported is derived by multiplying the amount of each payment by the gross profit ratio, which is the ratio of the total gross profit[8] to be realized to the total contract price.

EXAMPLE

Mr. Johnson sells a property to Ms. White for $250,000, where Ms. White pays $50,000 down and the remainder is payable in equal annual installments over the next five years, plus a sufficient amount of interest. Mr. Johnson's basis in the property is $180,000. The selling expenses that he pays are $5,000.

The gross profit on the sale is $65,000, which is calculated as the $250,000 sale price, minus the $180,000 basis and $5,000 of selling expenses. The gross profit ratio is 26%, which is calculated as the gross profit of $65,000 divided by the $250,000 sale price. Therefore, $10,400 of each annual $40,000 payment is a gain on the sale. Mr. Johnson must also report the interest received each year as ordinary interest income.

A few additional rules pertaining to installment sales are as follows:

- *Mortgage implications.* If the buyer under an installment arrangement takes on a property that is subject to a mortgage, taking on the mortgage is not considered a payment.
- *Subsequent price reduction.* If the parties later agree to a reduced selling price, this will alter the gross profit on the sale. When this happens, the gross profit ratio is only adjusted on remaining payments; there is no adjustment to the gain reported in earlier years.
- *Tradable obligations.* When the seller can readily convert a buyer's obligation to pay into cash, this constitutes constructive receipt of the cash, and so triggers reporting of the related amount of gain. This is usually the case only when the obligation is in the form of a registered bond that can be traded in a securities market (a rare circumstance). If the obligation is converted to cash, then there may be a gain or loss associated with the sale of the obligation.
- *Unstated interest.* If the sales agreement does not provide that the buyer will pay a stated amount of interest, then a part of each payment due after the first six months must include an interest component. This imputed interest is calculated according to the most recent IRS formulation and reduces the selling price, which in turn reduces the calculated gain.

Real Estate Investment Trusts

Thus far, we have talked about direct purchases of real estate. It is also possible to invest in a real estate investment trust (REIT), which invests in property. An REIT is a company that owns, operates, or finances income-generating property. Under this arrangement, investors can earn dividends from real estate without having to directly

---

[8] Gross profit is the selling price of a property minus its adjusted basis. Interest is not included in the selling price.

buy, operate, or finance any property. The returns from REITs are somewhere be-tween those generated by bonds and equities, though there are significant differences by individual REIT. For example, the returns from an REIT whose tenants are long-term, high-quality customers may approximate the returns from a bond portfolio, while the returns from an REIT whose tenants are more short-term will fluctuate to a greater extent, and so will approximate the returns from equities.

REITs tend to specialize in a specific real estate sector, such as apartment com-plexes, hotels, healthcare facilities, or warehouses, though some are diversified. The shares of many REITs are publicly traded, so you can easily buy and sell their shares. The shares of other REITs are registered with the Securities and Exchange Commis-sion, but are not traded on any stock exchanges; this means that it is more difficult to acquire or sell shares in these entities.

The shares of REITs can form a meaningful proportion of your investment port-folio, because they offer stable annual dividends, as well as the potential for long-term capital appreciation. They can also be considered a distinct asset class, and so can provide some diversification of your investment portfolio. However, the amount of capital appreciation can be less than you might experience with other asset classes. Also, some REITs have high management and transaction fees, which can cut into the dividends that you might otherwise receive.

Real Estate Investment Best Practices

There are several ways to improve the returns from your real estate investments. The following best practices apply to all aspects of the process of searching for, acquiring, operating, and selling real estate:

- *Buy in built-out areas.* Property values tend to hold up better in areas where there is minimal undeveloped land, because no additional units can be built.
- *Buy where property is owner-occupied.* Neighborhoods are more stable when a large proportion of the properties are occupied by their owners. This tends to increase property values, so try to purchase rental properties in these areas.
- *Look for high cost-benefit upgrades.* When searching for property, look for fixes that are relatively easy and inexpensive to complete, and for which ten-ants will be willing to tolerate a significant rent increase. Examples of these fixes are a new coat of paint, new flooring, modest landscaping improve-ments, and new hardware on cabinets and drawers.
- *Avoid properties with significant deferred maintenance.* When the current owner of a property has clearly deferred major maintenance on a building (such as replacing a roof), it is a good bet that other undisclosed maintenance must also be completed – which will eat up your cash reserves. These prop-erties should be avoided, even if the owner appears willing to accept a low price.
- *Avoid buying converted apartments.* Developers sometimes convert older apartment buildings into condominiums and then sell the units. While the fit and finish of these units might look quite nice, the underlying structure of the

building is old and probably in need of a substantial amount of maintenance – which triggers ongoing increases in the assessments charged to the property owners. They also tend to have poor sound proofing, which will annoy your tenants and increase their turnover rate.

- *Avoid scattered properties.* It can be quite difficult to personally manage a number of smaller properties scattered over a wide area, especially when these properties are in need of ongoing maintenance. A better approach is to concentrate your investing in a small number of larger properties, with professional on-site management.

- *Avoid distant investment areas.* Some parts of the country have occasionally been tagged as being hot real estate markets. Recent examples are Miami and Phoenix. If you do not live in these areas, it is not prudent to invest there, because you do not know the details of the market. It is generally better to concentrate on regions with which you have a greater degree of familiarity.

- *Review foreclosed properties extra carefully.* When a property owner walks away from a property, leaving it for the lender, there is a fair chance that the person did so because there were severe problems that would cost more to remediate than their equity in the property (such as asbestos remediation or a cracked slab). There may also be liens against the property. Yet another possibility is the absence of permits on changes made to the property. All of these issues can cost significant amounts to remediate. Consequently, be extra careful about reviewing foreclosed properties before submitting a bid to buy them.

- *Adopt a rent-raising strategy.* Do not impose large rent increases at one time, because it can trigger a tenant exodus. Instead, consider a series of incremental increases, which existing tenants are more likely to tolerate. Also, consider whether any cost-effective improvements to the property can justify a rent increase, such as updates to kitchens, bathrooms, common areas, and elevators.

- *Minimize tenant turnover.* Profits can be severely impacted when units remain empty after a tenant leaves. You will also have to expend significant amounts to advertise for new tenants, screen them, and pay commissions. To minimize tenant turnover, be highly responsive to tenant needs, keep the property in pristine condition, and encourage tenants to sign longer-term leases.

- *Replace marginal tenants.* Though we just advised you to retain your current tenants, this does not apply to your worst tenants – those who bother their neighbors, complain constantly, and damage the building. In these cases, view the end of their lease agreements as an opportunity not to renew, so that you can search for higher-quality tenants.

- *Emphasize curb appeal.* A good way to attract new tenants is to clean up the exterior of the property and ensure that it always looks better than the surrounding properties, perhaps by improving the landscaping. Getting interested prospects to enter the building is the first step in keeping the property full of tenants.

- *Look for cost reductions.* There may be ways to cut back on expenses in ways that do not impact the look of the property, and which tenants will not care about. For example, a drip irrigation system can reduce the cost of water, while an energy audit may highlight the possibility of using LED lighting or adding insulation to cut electricity costs. Or, consider aggregating your insurance needs for several properties into one policy, which can cut your total insurance cost.

- *Refinance the property*. Watch mortgage rates, and consider refinancing at a lower interest rate if rates fall sufficiently to offset the cost of the financing fees. Further, consider refinancing using a shorter mortgage term, such as 15 years, since these arrangements require much smaller interest payments in aggregate (though the monthly mortgage bill will be larger). Another possibility is to pay extra whenever you have some excess cash, which reduces the term of the mortgage and therefore the aggregate amount of interest paid.

- *Be ready to sell*. Regularly review the direction in which prices are going in the area surrounding your property, and be willing to sell if it appears that local conditions are causing your property to depreciate in value. For example, an increase in the crime rate can cause a sharp decline in local values. In these cases, it may be better to sell now, thereby freeing up the cash to purchase property elsewhere, where there is a better chance of appreciation. The overall strategy should be to shift from less desirable areas into more desirable ones in order to enhance your opportunities for property appreciation.

Summary

Real estate investing can be quite profitable. However, go back and read through the How to Acquire Real Estate section in this chapter. The narrative contains many comments about the large number of other investors who are also in the market, looking for the next great deal. In addition, do not count on hoodwinking an owner into selling a foreclosed property at a deep discount to the market price; owners are generally sophisticated, with a good knowledge of the value of their real estate holdings, and sufficient connections with real estate agents to sell their properties for close to the market price. In short, it can be difficult to acquire real estate for a great price. Your focus should be more on not paying more than the market price, and then relying on good operational skills and property appreciation to earn a profit over the long term.

Chapter 9
Investing in Alternative Investments

Introduction

We have covered the main forms of investment in the preceding chapters. In addition, there are several alternative investments that you might consider. As we point out in the descriptions of each one, they are generally not recommended. Instead, the preceding ownership investments are considered to be the best choices.

Call Options

Rather than buying stock outright, it is possible to purchase a *call option* that gives you the right, but not the obligation, to buy the stock at a predetermined price within a specific range of dates. For example, you might purchase a call option that allows you to buy the shares of ABC International for $100 per share for the next six months. If the share price were to ascend from its current $90 price to $120, then it would make sense to exercise the call option, buy the shares for $100 each, and immediately sell them for a $20 profit per share. Offsetting this profit would be the price of the call option and any brokerage commissions.

The problem with call options is that the price of the stock might not increase to a point where it makes sense to exercise the option. If so, the option will expire, and you will have lost the amount that you spent on the option. For this reason, investing in call options is speculative, and so should be avoided.

Put Options

A *put option* is a contract that gives its holder the right, but not the obligation, to sell stock at a strike price, before the option's expiration date. This means that you can force the counterparty to buy your shares at a specific price if the market price of the stock declines. If the price of your stock holding does not decline, then the option expires unused. Put options are a risk management technique that can be used to prevent the value of your investments from falling below a targeted level.

Put options are most valuable when you want to hold shares for an extended period of time in order to take advantage of lower capital gains tax rates, but want to avoid the risk of the share price falling in value before the holding period has been completed. These options have the same problem as call options, which is that you may pay for an option and then never use it.

Currencies

It is possible to invest in other currencies, usually those that are considered to be stable – such as the Japanese yen or the Swiss franc. The investment logic is that you should shift your cash out of currencies that are declining in value and into stable ones, in order to benefit from relative increases in value. When you need the funds, you can convert back into your home currency at a better exchange rate, realizing a gain. This is certainly an option when the government of your country is engaging in inflationary fiscal practices, such as spending more money than it is taking in via tax receipts, and especially when it is printing new money at a rate that exceeds the growth rate of the country. For this reason, the residents of high-inflation countries routinely shift their excess cash balances into other currencies.

However, if your country of residence is *not* suffering from high inflation, then the case in favor of investing in foreign currencies is substantially less credible. The problem is that exchange rates can be moved up or down by a variety of factors that are not remotely controllable, such as the impact of bad weather on a country's economy, or investor expectations regarding the newly-elected president of a country, or changes in the interest rate that are set by its central bank. In short, unless high inflation is a factor, it is generally best to avoid investing in other currencies.

Hedge Funds

A *hedge fund* pools the money of contributing investors and tries to achieve above-market returns through a wide variety of investment strategies. Larger investors are attracted to the higher returns advertised by hedge funds, though actual returns are not necessarily better than the average market rate of return. Hedge funds do not necessarily subscribe to a particular investment philosophy, so they can roam the investment landscape, looking for anomalies of all types to take advantage of. However, they usually develop investment strategies that are designed to generate gains, irrespective of movements in the stock market, either up or down.

Hedge funds typically do not accept small investments, with minimum contributions starting as high as $1 million. Hedge fund managers are compensated with a percentage of the total assets in the investment pool, as well as a percentage of all profits generated. For example, a fund manager could take 2% of all capital under management, as well as 20% of all profits earned. These are extremely high fees, and in many cases will result in a fund manager taking all excess returns generated. Therefore, placing funds in a lower-cost investment fund will typically generate a better return than what can be produced from a hedge fund.

Hedge fund investment strategies may include the following options:

- *Leverage strategy*. There may be a considerable quantity of leverage (that is, investing borrowed funds) to achieve outsized returns on a relatively small capital base. This presents the risk that losses on leveraged funds can be outsized, triggering massive losses for investors.
- *Short sales strategy*. Hedge funds may borrow shares and sell them, in the expectation that the price of a security will drop, after which they buy the securities on the open market and return the borrowed securities. This is a very risky strategy, since a share price increase can introduce potentially unlimited losses for investors.

- *Derivatives strategy.* Investments are made in any number of derivatives, which can pay off based on a vast number of possible underlying indices or other measures.

Because of the enhanced use of leverage, as well as other speculative strategies, there is a much higher probability of loss in a hedge fund than would be the case in a more traditional investment fund that only invests in the securities of well-established companies. The level of potential loss is accentuated by the common requirement that investments cannot be withdrawn from a hedge fund for a period of at least one year. This requirement is needed because some hedge fund investments cannot be easily liquidated to meet a cash withdrawal demand by an investor. The requirement also allows a hedge fund manager to employ longer-term investment strategies.

Hedge funds avoid oversight by the Securities and Exchange Commission (SEC) by only allowing investments by large institutions and accredited investors (individuals with a large net worth or income). This means that hedge funds do not have to report as much information to their investors or the SEC.

Note: The term "hedge" in the name "hedge fund" is a misnomer, since it seems to imply that a fund attempts to mitigate its risk. This term comes from the early days of hedge funds, when funds attempted to reduce the risk of securities price declines in a bear market by shorting securities. Nowadays, the pursuit of outsized returns is the primary goal, and that cannot usually be achieved while risk is also being hedged.

Venture Capital

A *venture capital* (VC) fund is a corporate entity that pools the cash contributions of multiple investors and institutions for investments in startup companies. It places select bets on start-up businesses that it expects to grow rapidly, and cashes out in five to ten years, when these investments have matured. Many of these start-up companies will fail, so a VC firm needs to place a few very high-return investments in order to offset the many investments that fail. This is a high-risk environment for the investor, for several reasons. First, your money will be tied up with the VC firm for a number of years. Second, you are relying on the VC's partners to make the right investments, which may not turn out to be the case. And third, VC firms charge high fees for their services – typically a 2% annual fee and a 20% performance fee. Given these concerns, venture capital investments are a not realistic choice for most investors. You should only consider it if you have substantial excess assets, and are willing to accept the possibility of major losses on your invested funds.

Precious Metals

Some investors like to keep a portion of their funds invested in precious metals, such as silver or gold. There is some natural demand for these metals, since they are used in manufacturing and jewelry. In addition, there is cultural demand for them in some countries, such as India, where maintaining stocks of gold is considered a reasonable investment strategy. In short, a baseline level of demand maintains a floor price for these metals, above which the market price may vary.

Investing in precious metals can yield a reasonable return during periods of uncertainty, such as when the inflation rate increases, or when there are wars. During these times, investors tend to buy more precious metals, which drives up demand and therefore its price. However, the long-term return on investment tends to be poor, and certainly lower than the other major investment classes. Rather than investing directly in precious metals, an alternative that may yield a better return is to invest in a fund that focuses on investments in companies that deal with precious metals. By doing so, you can benefit from increases in the value of these shares.

Given the relatively low long-term return on precious metals, it is advisable to allocate only a small part of your funds to this investment category.

> **Tip:** Do not buy gold immediately after there has been an economic shock (such as a war), since the event will have already driven up the price of gold as other investors pile into this asset class. Instead, maintain a modest stock of gold (if at all) over the long term, buying it strategically when prices are low.

Of all precious metals, the most problematic is an investment in gold, since its actual uses are relatively limited. In essence, people who fear a loss of value in other assets are attracted to gold, even though it historically has generated a relatively poor return on investment. This means that the decision to invest in gold is emotional – there is no quantitatively-derived reason to do so.

Works of Art

It is possible to purchase works of art and hold them for an extended period of time, hoping that they appreciate in value. This is certainly an option when you display the artwork for your own enjoyment. However, consider that more expensive works of art should be insured, and stored properly. Further, if you do not plan to display your artwork, then you will need to pay storage fees to a reputable art storage facility. A further consideration is that some artists never catch on with collectors, so their artwork does not appreciate in value – rather the reverse. In short, there are valid reasons why artwork will not appreciate in value – which presents a reasonable case for limiting your investments in this area.

> **Tip:** If a major art gallery is actively supporting an artist, or the artist's works are being prominently displayed by major museums, then there is a much better chance that the artist's prior works will increase in value over time.

Collectibles

You might choose to invest in *collectibles*, which are items worth more than they were originally sold for, due to their rarity or popularity. Examples of collectibles are antiques, toys, coins, comic books, rare books, and stamps. As long as there is a strong market for collectibles, the prices of these items will increase. However, these increases are only based on supply and demand. If collectors become less enamored of a certain type of collectible, then demand will weaken and its price will decline – perhaps catastrophically. In short, collectibles are only valuable to collectors – they do not actually generate value on their own.

There are other concerns with collectibles. First, you may need to pay for storage, insurance, and appraisal costs. Second, it is entirely possible that the item purchased turns out to be a forgery. Third, the quality of the piece may deteriorate over time, especially if you are using sub-par storage. Finally, and most importantly, the long-term return on most collectibles is quite poor. In short, unless you are an absolute expert in regard to a particular type of collectible and love to collect it irrespective of future returns, it rarely makes sense to pour resources into this area.

Raw Land

A possible investment option is purchasing raw land, on the grounds that there is a limited supply of it. The logic states that a limited supply and an ever-increasing population should result in long-term demand that will eventually drive up the price of the land. While this logic might initially appear sound, there are several good reasons to be wary of this investment. First, property taxes will likely apply, resulting in annual cash outflows. Second, some land has minimal prospects for future increases in value, perhaps because it is located far away from population centers, or the land quality is low, or access to it is restricted, or there are legal issues interfering with how it may be used[9]. Despite these issues, it may be possible to acquire land in order to generate revenue from it directly, perhaps from conducting farming or ranching operations, or perhaps through a mining operation. However, a substantial investment of both time and money is needed to start up these types of operations, and the outcome may very well be losses, rather than profits. In short, investing in raw land is generally not recommended, unless you are highly knowledgeable about whether a particular plot of land is likely to increase in value.

Given the absence of any recurring income and the presence of ongoing costs, an investment in raw land should be considered highly speculative. The investment looks even more speculative when you consider that a land investment may need to be held for many years before there is any prospect of a reasonable return from it.

Timberland Investments

A reasonable investment opportunity is the purchase and long-term holding of timberland. The return on investment is derived primarily from rotation, which is the time period from when trees are planted to when they are harvested. Rotation can cover many decades, so this is an extremely long-term play. In addition to the long-term nature of this investment, it is also subject to several risks, such as losses due to fires,

---

[9] A key legal issue that can interfere with land use is the presence of an easement that allows an unrelated party access to your land. Another concern is when a conveyance of mineral rights allows an unrelated party to extract minerals from your property for financial gain.

droughts, and high-wind events (derechos). In addition, the governing jurisdiction may place restrictions on the amount of tree harvesting that can be conducted. A final risk is that timber products are closely linked to the construction industry, which periodically goes through multi-year slumps; one of these slumps could send forest product prices into the cellar for a protracted period of time.

Offsetting the risks of owning timberland is (quite literally) the long-term growth of timber. Depending on the type of tree, it typically grows at a rate of 1% to 3% per year, so it increases in value over time. Therefore, if timber prices are currently low, a reasonable option is to delay harvesting to a later period, while the timber continues to grow.

Timberland can be purchased through an arrangement where a large forest products company sells off its own land and then enters into a long-term wood supply contract with the acquiring party. Another option is to work through a timberland investment management organization (TIMO), which provides acquisition advice to investors and then manages the property on their behalf. In exchange, the TIMO charges a management fee, as well as a percentage of any profits earned. Or, you may invest directly in a publicly-traded forest products company. Yet another option is to invest in a real estate investment trust that specializes in timberland investments.

Summary

It is generally not a good idea to allocate much money to alternative investments. Even though some people have experienced substantial returns in this area, the overall performance of this category tends to be rather low, especially when compared to a balanced portfolio of securities.

Chapter 10
Individual Retirement Accounts

Introduction

Individual retirement accounts (IRAs) are among the most heavily-used retirement vehicles in the United States. These accounts are designed to defer the recognition of income that has been contributed to an account, so that the income can be recognized during your retirement, when you are presumably in a lower tax bracket. In this chapter, we discuss the various types of IRAs, caps on contributions to them, the deductibility of these contributions, required minimum distributions, and several related topics.

Overview of Individual Retirement Accounts

The reporting requirements for a qualified retirement plan are substantial, so a smaller employer may not want to invest the amount of staff time and money in maintaining one. An alternative is to encourage employees to create their own personal retirement accounts. There are many types of these accounts, of which the more popular are noted in the following subsections.

Individual Retirement Account (IRA)

An individual retirement account is also referred to as a traditional IRA. This is an account that a person creates, and into which he or she can contribute the lower of total annual compensation or (as of 2025) $7,000 per year, or $8,000 for those at least 50 years old. Depending upon the circumstances, these contributions may be tax deductible for those employees with lower compensation levels. In addition, any income earned on the funds invested in it is shielded from taxation until withdrawn. A person can begin withdrawing funds from the account as of age 59½, and is required to begin doing so as of age 73. If a person does not withdraw the minimum required amount as of age 73, the penalty for not doing so is 50% of the amount that should have been withdrawn.

A variation on the concept is the individual retirement annuity. This account is opened by buying an annuity contract from a life insurance company. In order to be classified as an IRA, the owner's interest in the contract must be nonforfeitable. Further, the contract must provide that the owner cannot transfer any part of it to another person. There must also be flexible premiums, so that payments can be altered if the owner's compensation changes. Also, the contract must state that contributions cannot be more than the deductible amount for an IRA, and that any refunded premiums must be used to pay for future premiums or buy more benefits before the end of the year following the year in which a refund was received.

Roth IRA

This is similar to a traditional IRA account, except that the participant pays taxes on funds when they are contributed to the account, rather than when the funds are later withdrawn. By doing so, all interest earned subsequent to placing funds in the account is tax-free. You can withdraw funds from the account as of age 59½. Since there is no subsequent taxation of the earnings in a Roth IRA, there is no reason for the government to require participants to draw down these funds, so there is no minimum draw down, as was the case for a traditional IRA. Instead, no withdrawal is required from this account until your death. Once the account owner dies, the same minimum distribution rules that apply to traditional IRAs also apply to Roth IRAs.

The following table shows the scenarios under which it is possible to make contributions to a Roth IRA.

Ability to Contribute to a Roth IRA

Filing Status	Modified Adjusted Gross Income	Contribution Status
Married filing jointly	Less than $236,000	Up to $7,000 ($8,000 if age 50 or older)
	At least $236,000 but less than $246,000	Reduced contribution
	$246,000+	No contribution allowed
Married filing separately, and lived with spouse at any time during the year	Zero	Up to $7,000 ($8,000 if age 50 or older)
	More than zero but less than $10,000	Reduced contribution
	$10,000+	No contribution allowed
Single, head of household, or married filing separately and did not live with your spouse at any time during the year	Less than $150,000	Up to $7,000 ($8,000 if age 50 or older)
	At least $150,000 but less than $165,000	Reduced contribution
	$165,000+	No contribution allowed

IRA and Roth IRA Comparison

Some of the differences and similarities between traditional and Roth IRAs are noted in the following exhibit.

Comparison of Traditional and Roth IRAs

Features	Traditional IRA	Roth IRA
Who is allowed to contribute?	Anyone with taxable compensation	Anyone with taxable compensation and a modified adjusted gross income below a predetermined cap
Can contributions be deducted?	Qualifying contributions are deductible	Contributions are not deductible
How much can be contributed?	The combined amount for both IRAs is the smaller of $6,500 (or $7,500 for someone age 50 or older), or one's taxable compensation for the year.	
What is the contribution deadline?	The tax return filing deadline, not including any extensions.	
When can money be withdrawn?	Money can be withdrawn at any time.	
Is a minimum distribution required?	The account owner must begin taking distributions by April 1 following the year in which he or she turned age 73, and by December 31 of subsequent years.	Not required for the original owner of the account.
Are withdrawals taxable?	All deductible contributions and earnings that are withdrawn are taxable. If a withdrawal is made prior to age 59½, a 10% tax may be imposed.	A qualified distribution is not taxable. A distribution is qualified when it is made after the five-year period beginning with the first tax year for which a contribution was made to the account, *and* the distribution was made after reaching age 59½, or was made due to being disabled, or for a first-time home purchase, or was made to a beneficiary or estate due to the account owner's death. Otherwise, a 10% tax may be imposed.

In the last row of the preceding exhibit, we noted a number of situations in which a distribution from a Roth IRA is considered to be a qualified distribution. The flowchart in the following exhibit clarifies when this is the case.

Qualified Distribution Criteria for a Roth IRA

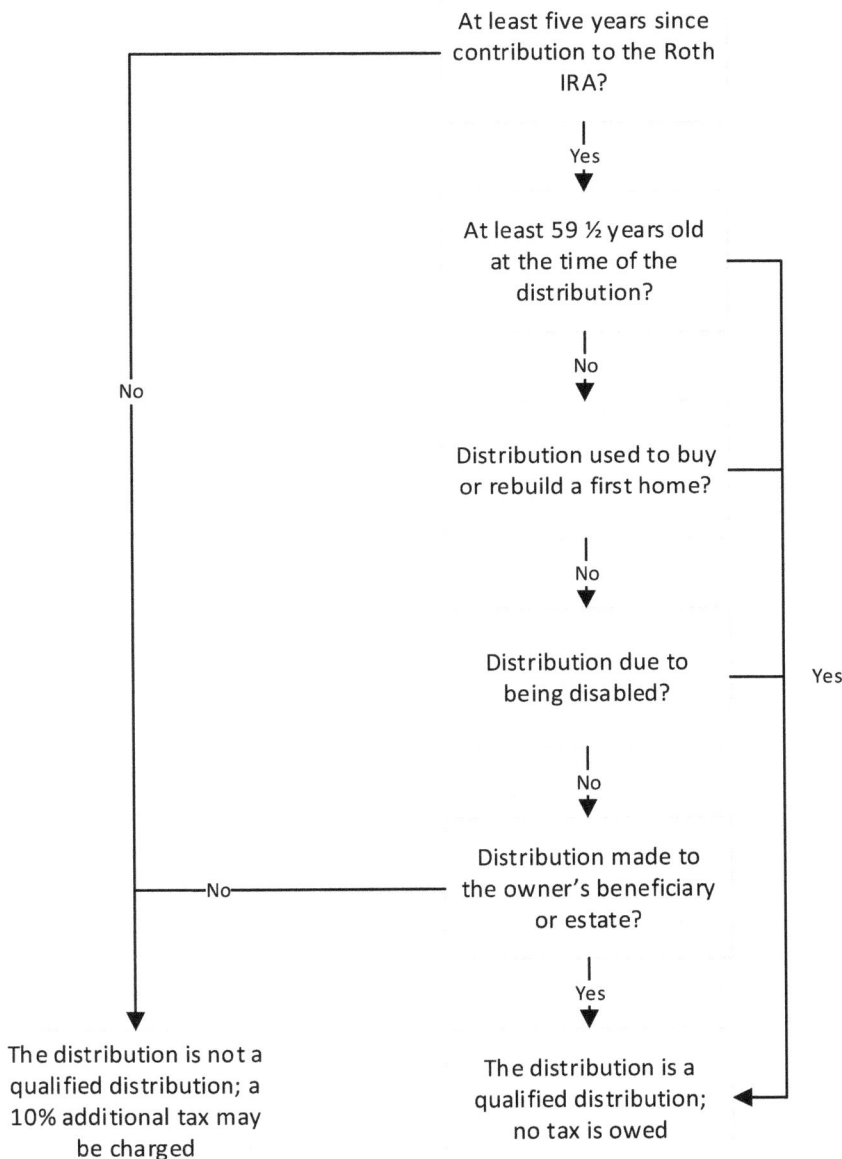

At least five years since contribution to the Roth IRA?

| Yes

At least 59 ½ years old at the time of the distribution?

| No

Distribution used to buy or rebuild a first home?

| No

Distribution due to being disabled?

| No

Distribution made to the owner's beneficiary or estate?

| Yes

No

Yes

The distribution is not a qualified distribution; a 10% additional tax may be charged

The distribution is a qualified distribution; no tax is owed

Rollover IRA

When you leave a business where you have funds in a qualified pension plan, the best options are to either leave the funds in the plan, roll them into the qualified plan of the new employer, or roll them into a rollover IRA. This last option is an IRA account that is specifically designed to accept funds from qualified pension plans. Since many people have multiple employers during their careers, many with qualified pension plans, it makes sense to consolidate the funds in these accounts into a rollover IRA.

Savings Incentive Match Plan for Employees (SIMPLE)

As the acronym implies, this is a simplified retirement plan under which both the employer and employee can make contributions to an IRA account. It is funded through a pre-tax reduction of employee gross pay. The maximum annual contribution to a SIMPLE account (as of 2025) was $16,500 and $20,000 for those at least 50 years old. A SIMPLE plan can only be created by an employer having fewer than 100 employees, or which has employed an average of 100 or fewer employees in either of the two preceding years. If a business subsequently increases its employment, it can still operate a SIMPLE plan as long as it does not employ an average of 100 or more people in a subsequent year. This plan requires the employer to match each employee's salary reduction contribution on a dollar-for-dollar basis up to 3% of the employee's compensation. A variation is the nonelective contribution, where the employer can choose to make a 2%-of-compensation contribution on behalf of each eligible employee, even if the employees do not elect to make a salary deduction into their IRA accounts.

EXAMPLE

Alvin, an employee of Universal Routers, earned $60,000 and elected to defer 5% of his salary by contributing it to a SIMPLE IRA. The company makes a standard 3% match to all such contributions. This means that Alvin contributes $3,000 to the account (calculated as $60,000 × 5%), while the company contributes $1,800 (calculated as $60,000 × 3%).

If a participant wants to withdraw funds from a SIMPLE account before age 59½, the penalty is 10% of the distribution, or 25% if the withdrawal occurs within two years of beginning participation in the plan.

When a SIMPLE plan is set up, a separate IRA account must be created for each participating employee. Participating employees are those who received at least $5,000 in compensation during any two years preceding the current calendar year, and who are reasonably expected to receive at least that much during the current calendar year.

Simplified Employee Pension (SEP) IRA

This plan is designed for the self-employed person, but can be extended to all types of business entities. A SEP IRA can only be created if there is no qualified retirement plan already in place. Contributions to a SEP IRA are protected from income taxes until such time as they are withdrawn from the account. Participants may begin withdrawing funds from the account as of age 59½, and must make required minimum distributions once they reach age 73. The total contribution to a SEP IRA cannot exceed the lesser of 25% of a participant's annual compensation or $70,000 (as of 2025).

These contribution levels make the SEP IRA one of the best ways to protect a substantial amount of funds from taxation.

EXAMPLE

Martha earned $48,000 in 2025. The maximum contribution she can make to her SEP IRA is $12,000 (calculated as 25% × $48,000).

EXAMPLE

Mary earned $300,000 in 2025. The maximum contribution she can make to her SEP IRA is $70,000, since that is the maximum allowable contribution for 2025.

Someone who is eligible for a SEP IRA must be at least 21 years old, has worked for the business in at least three of the past five years, and has received at least $650 of compensation from the business in the past year.
Contributions to a SEP IRA must be in cash; contributions of property are not allowed.

> **Note:** If SEP contributions exceed the annual deduction limit, the excess can be carried forward and used in a later year. However, an excess contribution can be subject to a 10% excise tax.

Ability to Contribute to an IRA

Anyone can make contributions to a traditional IRA if they received taxable compensation during the year. This is the case even if a taxpayer is already covered by another retirement plan. However, when there *is* another retirement plan, it may not be possible to deduct all contributions made to the IRA.

As long as both spouses in a marriage are earning compensation, each one can open an IRA. However, they cannot both participate in the same IRA; each person must maintain a separate account. If the two file a joint return, then only one spouse needs to have compensation for both of them to contribute to an IRA.

> **Note:** The compensation from which IRA contributions can be made include wages, salaries, commissions, alimony, combat pay, and graduate study income. It does *not* include earnings from property, interest and dividend income, pension or annuity income, deferred compensation, or any amounts excluded from taxable income.

Even someone participating in an employer-sponsored retirement plan (such as a SIMPLE IRA or SEP IRA) can contribute to a traditional IRA or Roth IRA. However, as noted in a following section, these contributions may not be deductible.

Contributions to an IRA can be made at any time during the year, or by the due date for filing one's return for that year, not including extensions. For example, a contribution made for 2023 must usually be made by April 15, 2024. If a contribution is made to an IRA between January 1 and April 15, the account sponsor must be told the year to which the contribution is to be applied. If the account owner does not make this designation, then the account sponsor will report to the IRS that it was made for the current year.

Caps on IRA Contributions

The contribution caps for singles and spouses are noted in the following sub-sections, as well as the treatment of excess contributions.

Contribution Caps for Singles

The general cap rule on IRA contributions is the smaller of a person's taxable compensation or $7,000 ($8,000 if the person is at least 50 years old).

EXAMPLE

Alvin is 37 years old and single. He earned $39,000 in the past year. His IRA contribution is capped at $7,000 in that year.

Margot is 25 and single. She earned $2,000 while working on a part-time basis in the past year. Her IRA contribution is capped at $2,000 (her compensation) in that year.

If a person invests in an individual retirement annuity, then the amount that can be contributed towards its cost is capped at $7,000 per year ($8,000 if the person is at least 50 years old). A larger contribution will disqualify the annuity contract.

Contribution Caps for Spouses

Both spouses can contribute to their own separate IRAs when they file a joint return and have taxable compensation. The most that can be contributed for the year to a spouse's IRA is the lesser of the following amounts:

- $7,000 (or $8,000 if the person is at least 50 years old); or
- The total compensation includible in the gross income of both spouses, less the other spouse's IRA contribution for the year to a traditional IRA and any contributions for the year to a Roth IRA on behalf of your spouse.

It does not matter which spouse earned the income. These rules mean that the maximum contribution that can be made for the year by both spouses is $16,000, if both are at least 50 years old.

EXAMPLE

Victoria marries Albert. Albert has no taxable income (being a medical student), while Victoria earns $300,000 a year as an investment banker. Both are in their 20s. Victoria plans to contribute $7,000 to a traditional IRA. If they file a joint return, each one can contribute $7,000 to a traditional IRA. This is because Albert, who earns no income, can add Victoria's compensation, reduced by the amount of her IRA contribution ($293,000) to his own compensation to calculate his maximum contribution to a traditional IRA.

If a person contributes less than the maximum amount to a traditional IRA in one year, it is not possible to contribute an additional amount after the due date of that year's tax return in order to make up the difference.

Excess Contributions

When an excess contribution is made to a traditional IRA, it is subject to a 6% tax. This tax must be paid every year on excess amounts that remain in the account at the end of the tax year. No tax is due as long as the excess amount and any interest earned on it is withdrawn from the account by the date the tax return for that year is due, including extensions.

EXAMPLE

Irma has mistakenly made an excess contribution to her IRA of $1,000. She does not withdraw these funds by the time her tax return is due, so she owes a $60 (6%) tax on the excess $1,000.

Deductibility of IRA Contributions

Contributions to a traditional IRA can be deducted if neither spouse is covered by a retirement plan at work. However, these contributions may be limited if either spouse is covered by a retirement plan at work and their income exceeds certain threshold levels. When a couple files a joint return, the deduction is limited to the lesser of the following:

- $7,000 (or $8,000 if the spouse with the lower compensation is age 50 or older); or
- The total compensation in the couple's gross income, reduced by all of the following:
  - The IRA deduction of the spouse with the greater compensation
  - Any designated nondeductible contribution for the spouse with the greater compensation
  - Any contributions for a Roth IRA for the spouse with the greater compensation

As just noted, the deduction that can be taken for contributions to a traditional IRA depends on whether there was any coverage during the year by an employer retirement plan. When this is the case, the deduction may be reduced or eliminated. The deduction begins to decline when a person's income rises above a designated threshold amount, and is cancelled when it attains a higher threshold amount. The following table contains the basic rules for the amount of the deduction that can be taken.

Deductibility of Traditional IRA Contributions (Coverage by Retirement Plan)

Filing Status	Modified Adjusted Gross Income	Deduction Status
Single or head of household	$79,000 or less	Full deduction
	$79,001 to $89,000	Partial deduction
	$89,000+	No deduction
Married filing jointly	$126,000 or less	Full deduction
	$126,001 to $146,000	Partial deduction
	$146,000+	No deduction
Married filing separately	Less than $10,000	Partial deduction
	$10,000+	No deduction

EXAMPLE

Florence is 31 years old and single. She was covered by her retirement plan at work during the current year. Her modified AGI for the year is $92,000. Florence makes a $7,000 contribution to her traditional IRA for the year. Because she is covered by an employer retirement plan and her modified adjusted gross income exceeds the $89,000 threshold, she cannot deduct the contribution. Instead, it is classified as a nondeductible contribution.

All nondeductible contributions must be reported on Form 8606, *Nondeductible IRAs*. If these contributions are not reported on the form, then all distributions from the IRA will be taxed.

The following additional items pertain to deductibility:

- Contributions made to a Roth IRA are not deductible.
- Trustee's administrative fees that are billed separately in relation to an IRA are not deductible.
- Broker's commissions are considered part of an IRA contribution, and so are deductible.

Allowable Distributions

It is entirely allowable to take distributions from an IRA at any time, and there is no need to show hardship in order to do so. When a distribution is taken, the amount will appear in the account owner's taxable income. Depending on the circumstances, these distributions may be subject to an early distribution penalty, as described in the next section.

Early Distribution Penalties

Though a traditional IRA is designed to confer tax advantages on an account owner, these advantages can be more than offset by additional taxes and penalties if account usage rules are not followed. In particular, if a distribution is taken before an account owner is 59½ years old, it may be subject to a 10% additional tax. However, there are several exceptions that can be used to avoid the 10% tax, which are as follows:

- The recipient has unreimbursed medical expenses that are more than 7.5% of his or her adjusted gross income.
- The distributions made are not more than the cost of one's medical insurance, due to a period of unemployment.
- The recipient is totally and permanently disabled.
- The recipient is the beneficiary of an account owner who dies before reaching age 59½.
- The recipient is receiving distributions in the form of an annuity, as long as there is at least one distribution per year.
- The distributions do not exceed the amount of one's qualified higher education expenses. These expenses can be for the recipient or a spouse, children or grandchildren, and must be for tuition, fees, books, supplies, and equipment related to educational activities.
- The distributions are being used to acquire or build a first home, and do not exceed $10,000.
- The distribution is a qualified reservist distribution, where the recipient was called to active duty for a period of more than 179 days.
- The distribution is a qualified birth or adoption distribution, if made during the one-year period beginning on the date of birth or adoption, and for an amount not to exceed $5,000.

These exceptions also apply to distributions from a Roth IRA account.

EXAMPLE

Andrea is 40 years old. She receives a $4,500 distribution from her traditional IRA account. She does not qualify for any of the exceptions to the 10% additional tax, so the $4,500 is classified as an early distribution. Andrea must include the $4,500 in her gross income in the year in which the distribution was made, paying income tax on this amount. She must also pay an additional $450 tax (calculated as $4,500 distribution × 10% additional tax).

Further, a distribution taken from a SIMPLE IRA within the first two years of participation will be subject to an additional 25% tax.

Taxability of IRA Interest

The interest earned on funds stored in an IRA are not taxed in the year earned. Instead, the tax on this interest is deferred until a distribution is made from the account. Therefore, this interest is not reported to the IRS as tax-exempt interest.

Required Minimum Distributions

A minimum withdrawal is required for a traditional IRA, SIMPLE IRA and SEP IRA by April 1 of the year following the calendar years in which the account owner reaches age 73. This age is reduced to 70½ years for those born before July 1, 1949. The basic rules associated with these withdrawals are as follows:

- It is allowable to withdraw more than the minimum required amount.
- There is no exception from the required minimum withdrawals for those who are still working.
- Withdrawals must be included in taxable income except for any funds that had already been taxed, or which can be received tax-free. No withdrawal is required from a Roth IRA account until the death of the owner, since the funds placed in the account were already taxed.
- Subsequent withdrawals must be made by December 31 of each year. For the first year following the year when an account owner reaches the triggering age a distribution is required by April 1, followed by another withdrawal by December 31.

EXAMPLE

Emily reaches age 73 on September 15, 2024. She must receive her 2024 required minimum distribution by April 1, 2025, based on her 2024 year-end balance. Emily must receive her 2025 required minimum distribution by December 31, 2025, based on her 2025 year-end balance.

The required minimum distribution in each year is the account balance at the end of the immediately preceding calendar year, divided by the distribution period stated on the IRS's Uniform Lifetime Table for the account owner's age.

Qualified Charitable Distributions

A qualified charitable distribution is a distribution from an IRA that would otherwise have been taxable, which is paid directly to a qualified charity. A further requirement is that the qualified charity must issue an acknowledgement of the contribution that would normally be issued for a donor to claim a deduction for a charitable donation.

These distributions can be used to satisfy the required minimum distribution from an IRA. A qualified charity is one that is eligible to receive tax-free donations.

EXAMPLE

Charity Do-Right (sister of Dudley) is required to make a $7,000 required minimum distribution from her IRA in the current year. She distributes $6,000 from the IRA directly to a qualified charity, and then has to withdraw another $1,000 to satisfy the minimum distribution requirement.

The maximum annual exclusion for qualified charitable distributions is $108,000. Any distributions to a qualified charity that exceed this amount are included in one's taxable income. If a joint return is being filed, then each spouse can exclude up to $108,000 per year.

Summary

An IRA can be quite a useful way to avoid the recognition of income until your retirement. However, an IRA must be used within the rules, or else taxes and penalties could offset or even exceed this benefit. In particular, you should be cognizant of the income levels at which contributions are no longer deductible, avoid early distributions, and be sure to take the required minimum distribution. In particular, the required minimum distribution *must* be observed, or else you could be hit with a 50% excise tax.

Chapter 11
Socially Responsible Investing

Introduction

Some investors believe that there are ethical issues associated with where they invest their money. This means that they may refuse to invest in certain companies or perhaps in entire industries. For example, they may choose not to invest in tobacco companies, due to the negative health consequences of their products, or in oil and gas companies, due to the carbon dioxide emissions associated with their products. Or, they may choose not to invest in firms that are perceived to be treating employees unfairly, or avoiding taxes, or operating in countries with autocratic governments. In this chapter, we cover some of the issues associated with socially responsible investing.

ESG Investing

Socially responsible investing is generally considered to encompass ESG investing, which is short for environmental, social, and governance. There are many investment funds that set up ESG classification criteria for their investments, and offer to clients a restricted list of companies that qualify under these criteria for investment. This is done not only to attract those investors who are concerned about ESG issues, but also so that the fund managers can charge extra fees for their ESG monitoring services.

The filtering criteria for ESG investing are roughly the same for all ESG funds, and are as follows:

- *Environmental filters.* Any companies whose activities or products harm the environment. This may include chemical producers, mining firms, and emitters of methane or carbon dioxide (such as cement plants).
- *Social filters.* Any companies whose activities or products are considered to be unethical. This may include arms manufacturers, casinos, alcohol or tobacco firms, or pornography producers or distributors. Conversely, a filter could look for positive values, such as high-quality employment, the construction of affordable housing, micro-financing, and significant contributions to local communities.
- *Governance filters.* Any companies whose governance structure is poor, such as having an in-bred board of directors, or which are frequently cited by regulators for violating regulations.

The application of these filters is clearly subjective, so the ESG inclusions or exclusions used by various funds will differ, depending on the exact nature of their filters and how these filters are interpreted.

There is a counter-argument to those who only invest in environmentally-friendly businesses. That argument states that the avoidance of these businesses drives up their cost of capital, so that they have less funding available. When this is the case, an organization is more likely to concentrate its investments on its highest-return activities, which tend to be those that have the most negative impact on the environment. Consequently, not investing in these businesses may actually increase their propensity to cause environmental damage.

Thematic Investments

Some investment funds are set up to provide investors with investment choices that are targeted at specific goals, such as clean water, or carbon absorption technologies, or sustainable fish farming. These funds are looking for emerging and established companies that engage in activities that investors want, while also providing the prospect of a good return. A great deal of effort is required to search for and screen these companies, so thematic funds will charge a fee for this service. In addition, many of the companies included in these funds are rather small or operate in emerging markets, so there is a greater risk of failure. Also, there tend to be a relatively small number of companies in these funds, so you will be at risk of making an undiversified investment. All of these issues represent investment risks.

One focus of these funds is on sustainable investing. This type of investing directs investment capital to businesses that do not exhaust the world's resources or cause irreversible damage to its climate. With this goal in mind, a fund will only make a company's securities available to its investors if the firm is actively working on reducing its resource consumption, reducing its emissions of pollutants, and even assisting its customers in reducing their environmental impact on the planet. A thematic fund will typically publicize its ranking and screening criteria for these factors, which investors can use to decide whether they want to invest in the fund.

Those who support thematic investing argue that these investments will generate above-average returns, since the companies included in these funds are better prepared for the future, being less subject to its environmental vagaries and the related governmental regulations that will likely arise. The offsetting arguments are that the fund will charge a higher fee for its services (cutting into any returns), and that these funds are so restricted in the range of companies offered that they are bound to not include some outliers that would otherwise have generated outsized returns for the investor. In short, it is difficult to objectively state that the returns from these funds will be exceptionally high or low.

> **Tip:** Check the relevant tax regulations; Congress occasionally passes legislation that can provide tax benefits if you make certain types of investments in environmental activities.

Summary

You may have an interest in socially responsible investing, but are uncertain about whether the associated returns will be less than what you are used to. A good way to edge into this type of investing is to identify the investment themes that are of most concern to you, and invest a modest part of your cash in the relevant thematic funds. You can then make adjustments over time, based on how your interests change and whether you are making sufficient returns on these investments.

Chapter 12
The Role of Insurance
in Wealth Management

Introduction

You should certainly consider whether to obtain insurance as part of your wealth management plan. There are several ways in which insurance can be used, which are as follows:

- To protect against property damage
- To protect against the loss of income due to poor health
- To protect your family from liabilities in the event of your death
- To protect against outlasting your financial resources
- To offset the cost of estate taxes

We will explore the relevant types of insurance that can provide these protections in the following pages.

Property Insurance

This policy protects against the loss of physical assets. The cost can be substantial, if you own one or more expensive homes and other assets. If you have used mortgages to acquire assets, the lienholders will require that property insurance be purchased in order to protect their interests in the assets. This is usually considered essential insurance, since it provides coverage of what may be a large part of your net worth.

Types of Property

The coverage given by property insurance applies to two types of property, which are real property and personal property. *Real property* is defined as any property that is directly attached to the land, plus land itself. Examples are homes and storage units, as well as improvements to these structures. *Personal property* is defined as being movable, and so may include furniture and fixtures, vehicles, and collectibles.

Policy Inclusions

There are three different classifications of damage to property that may be covered by property insurance, depending on the type of coverage purchased. The three classifications are as follows:

- *Causes of loss – basic form.* Coverage is provided when the causes of loss include fire, lightning, windstorms, hail, riots, damage by aircraft or vehicles, smoke, explosion, vandalism, volcanism, a sinkhole collapse, or discharge from an automatic sprinkler system.

- *Causes of loss – broad form.* Coverage is provided for all of the perils just noted for the basic form, as well as for falling objects, weight of snow, ice, or sleet, and water damage.
- *Causes of loss – special form.* Coverage is provided for all types of accidental loss, unless there is a specific exclusion.

Damage due to flooding and earthquakes is typically excluded from all property insurance policies, but can be added back as a separate endorsement to a policy.

Property is covered if it is located within 100 feet of the insured premises. Additional coverage can be obtained that provides coverage at other locations, as well as for newly acquired or constructed property that is obtained after the effective date of the policy.

Policy Exclusions

A number of items are specifically excluded from a property insurance policy. Depending on the policy, exclusions may encompass the following:

- *Animals.* This depends on who owns the animals and how they are being stored. For example, horses boarded by the insured entity may be covered if they are kept in a stable.
- *Cash and securities.* This includes bills and coins, bonds, and equity securities.
- *Land and land improvements.* This includes roadways, lawns, bridges, underground pipes, patios, roadways, pilings, and parking lots.
- *Plants and outdoor property.* This includes crops, lawns, shrubs, trees, antennas and signs.
- *Vehicles.* This exclusion applies except when the vehicles are being held for sale or stored.
- *Covered elsewhere.* This includes property that is more specifically addressed under another insurance policy.

Additional Coverages

There are a number of additional coverages that can be added to property insurance. They only apply to specific circumstances, and so may only be needed for shorter periods of time. If so, be sure to remove them during the next coverage period, so that you are not needlessly paying for inapplicable coverage. Several additional coverages are:

- *Buildings under construction.* A building that is under construction may not be covered by property insurance. This situation can be remedied by adding an endorsement to the standard property insurance policy. The endorsement should cover materials, equipment, and temporary structures adjacent to the work site. For example, a general conflagration could consume nearby building materials and the on-site trailer used by the construction staff.

- *Debris removal.* This coverage pays for the cost of removing debris from a damaged or destroyed building, up to a maximum cap. This typically does not include the cost to remediate pollution caused by whatever caused the property damage. This can be useful coverage when property is extensive, such as a large home.
- *Fire department charges.* This coverage reimburses the insured entity for the amount of any service charges imposed by the local fire department for sending its equipment to a covered location. This coverage can be useful when local ordinances require such charges to property holders by the fire department.
- *Pollutant clean-up.* This coverage pays for the cost to remove pollutants from the premises if the pollution was caused by the event that damaged the property. There is a cap on this coverage.
- *Property preservation.* This coverage addresses any damage to property while it is being transported to a safe location or being stored there. This coverage can make sense if high-value items are being insured, such as artwork.

Valuation Issues

The insurance pays for the rebuilding of damaged or destroyed real property. Further, it pays for the value or replacement cost of any lost or damaged personal property. If a policy is paying for the value of an asset, this means the replacement cost of the asset, less depreciation. Thus, an older asset will have a significantly lower replacement value than a new asset.

The depreciation concept can seriously reduce the amount of a payment related to a loss, since the insurer reduces the value of the damaged asset by an estimate of its prior use.

Remedial Activities

There can be arguments over the number and types of assets for which reimbursement is claimed. To bolster your case, it is useful to take the following steps:

- *Record contents.* Create a record of the contents of your homes, including digital photos, which can be used to substantiate a claim. This record will soon be out of date, so schedule an annual update of the report. A variation on the concept is to take a video of the homes, to which can be appended an audio commentary. A video takes less time to complete than a formal written record.
- *Store records safely.* Maintain all documentation pertaining to the purchase cost of assets in a fire-proof safe, or in a secure off-site location. It may make sense to maintain a duplicate set of records in an alternate location.

In addition, you should take action to prevent further damage to property, once a loss event has occurred. For example, if your home's roof is destroyed, you should take prompt action to protect the contents of the building from further weather-related damage. If not, the insurer may deny claims related to subsequent damage to the home's contents.

> **Tip:** It is quite common to under-insure property, because you have underestimated its replacement cost. To guard against this, schedule an annual meeting with your insurance agent to review your asset replacement costs.

Life Insurance

The primary use of life insurance is to pay for the living expenses of a spouse or your children. This is a particular concern when your spouse does not work or earns a significantly lower wage than you, as well as when the children are still many years from becoming adults, when they can support themselves. An additional use of life insurance is that it can provide the cash needed to pay for any debts outstanding at the time of your death, as well as to pay funeral costs or any estate taxes. In these situations, a relatively large-value policy will be needed.

> **Tip:** Check the terms of any outstanding loans, to see if any of them require immediate repayment in the event of your death. If this is the case, have sufficient life insurance to pay off these loans.

A particularly good use for life insurance is when you have a large estate that will be subject to estate taxes, and which is comprised of mostly non-liquid assets (such as your ownership interest in a business). In these cases, it may be necessary to sell the non-liquid assets quickly, in order to pay the estate taxes. To give your beneficiaries the option to retain control over your assets, it makes sense to obtain sufficient life insurance to pay the expected amount of the estate taxes. Conversely, if the estate already has sufficient cash on hand to pay estate taxes, then there will be no need for life insurance to deal with this issue.

Another possible use for life insurance arises when you own a business, and it depends on you for a large part of its cash flow (perhaps because you are great at sales!). If you want the business to stay in operation after your death, consider how much additional cash it will need to stay in operation until a replacement for you can be found. Or, think about how much cash it will need until a buyer can be found for the business. This should constitute the amount of life insurance you will need.

Conversely, if your situation does not fall into the classifications just stated, then there is no need for life insurance. For example, the typical person whose children have grown up and whose estate falls below the estate tax threshold has no need for life insurance. If there is a limited need for life insurance, then only purchase enough for the indicated need; otherwise, you are wasting money on this insurance.

Varieties of Life Insurance

There are two main types of life insurance. A term policy only provides coverage for a set amount of time, while there are several varieties of permanent insurance that cannot be cancelled by the insurer, unless the associated premiums are not paid on time. It is possible to purchase both term and permanent insurance with a single up-front lump sum payment.

The essential concept behind term life insurance is that it pays out a specific amount of cash if you die during the predefined period when the policy is still in force. It is also the least expensive form of life insurance, since it provides no other benefit. It is relatively inexpensive to obtain if you are young, since the probability of your death is quite low at that time. Consequently, it is an excellent choice when you are young and have young children to protect. As you get older, the price of term insurance increases, since the risk of your death goes up with age. Given the gradual increase in the cost of this insurance, people tend to drop coverage as they age.

EXAMPLE

Wilma purchases a term life insurance policy that will pay out $250,000 if she dies within the next ten years. She dies ten years and one day later, so the policy is no longer in force and the insurer is not obligated to pay out any funds.

A permanent insurance policy automatically rolls forward year after year. The amount you pay for the policy each year is the same. Given that the risk of a payout increases for the insurer each year, you are paying more than would be the case with a term insurance policy during the early years of a permanent policy, and less than would be required for a term insurance policy later in life. The early excess payment is invested by the insurer in order to generate returns that can be used to pay for the eventual payout. Or, if you choose to end the policy, you can obtain this excess amount, which is known as its *cash surrender value*. If the returns on excess policy payments are left with the insurer, then they are not taxable. Conversely, if you choose to cash in the policy, then the cash surrender value is subject to tax.

There are three variations on the permanent insurance concept, which are as follows:

- *Whole life insurance*. This is the most basic type of permanent insurance, providing a fixed amount of uncancellable coverage in exchange for the same payment amount, year after year.
- *Universal life insurance*. This is the same as whole life insurance, but also provides some flexibility in altering the amount of the premiums paid and the death benefit.
- *Variable life insurance*. This has the same benefits as universal life insurance, but also lets you invest in a variety of investment options. The value of your policy may fluctuate as the value of your chosen investments change over

time, which means that the associated death benefit could change substantially.

A variation on the life insurance concept is the *first-to-die policy*. Under this arrangement, several people are insured under one policy, with the insurer paying out when the first person dies. This is useful for business partnerships, where the surviving partners need the cash to buy out the beneficiaries' interest in the business. Alternatively, the funds could be used to hire people to replace the owner who has died. It is most common for the business to pay for the related insurance premiums, rather than the insured parties.

EXAMPLE

Able, Bascom and Chanteria start up a new business. Their partnership agreement mandates that, in the event of the death of one of them, the other two partners can buy out the interest of that person. The firm has little excess cash, since it is using all available funds to expand the business. To deal with this situation, the business purchases a first-to-die policy that covers the three of them. The firm acquires sufficient coverage to pay off double the share of one partner, on the assumption that the value of the business will double. Bascom dies five years later, so the insurer pays the business the full amount of the policy. Able and Chanteria use the money to buy out Bascom's interest in the firm, paying his beneficiaries. There is some residual cash from the policy, which is retained as working capital. Able and Chanteria are now 50-50 owners of the business.

Annuities

An *annuity* is an investment option that provides you with a guaranteed income for the duration of your retirement. When purchased, an annuity is designed to pay out over a specific period of time, and in a fixed amount. This is a good option when you are concerned about outliving your accumulated savings.

Under an annuity plan, you select an annuity type and then purchase the plan from an insurer. The insurance company invests the payment, so that the account earns interest on top of the original invested amount for the duration of the contract. Once you decide to start collecting payments from the annuity, the insurer makes a series of scheduled payments back to you. Here are several types of annuities that you could purchase:

- *Immediate annuity*. Under this arrangement, the payout starts shortly after you make the premium payment to the insurer.
- *Deferred annuity*. Under this arrangement, the payout starts as of a future date, which may be many years away.
- *Fixed annuity*. Under this arrangement, the payout is based on an amount that is guaranteed in the underlying contract. The insurer bears the risk of not earning a sufficient amount on your premium payment to make this fixed payment amount.

- *Indexed payment*. Under this arrangement, the insurer provides a guaranteed return, along with the option of sharing in any additional investment earnings.
- *Variable annuity*. Under this arrangement, the payout will vary, so there is no guaranteed payment. A variety of charges will be applied to your premium and any investment earnings, after which the residual amount is paid out.

There are several downsides to annuities. One is the large commission paid to the person who sells you the annuity – which is taken from your premium payment before it has a chance to begin earning any interest income. Another concern is that the insurer will apply a number of fees to the plan, which reduces the amount of your eventual payouts. Consequently, some investors prefer to invest their own funds, rather than shifting this task over to an insurer.

Summary

Life insurance tends to be more necessary earlier in your life, when your children are still minors. Once they become adults and can earn a living themselves, there is less need for life insurance. It is also less of a concern once you have retired, and presumably have built up a fairly large cash reserve. Consequently, it makes sense to periodically review your life insurance situation and adjust the amount of your life insurance policies.

An annuity is most useful when you want to be assured of a steady income right through your retirement years. However, there are costs associated with these products that might lead you to invest cash yourself to obtain the same outcome.

Chapter 13
Charitable Contributions

Introduction

You may be able to claim a deduction for charitable contributions, thereby preserving a portion of your wealth. In this chapter, we describe the contributions that qualify for a deduction, the types of organizations that can receive these deductions, how to value donated property, and several related topics.

The Nature of a Charitable Contribution

A *charitable contribution* is a donation or gift to, or for the use of, a qualified organization. It is made voluntarily, without getting anything of equal value in exchange.

Qualified Charitable Organizations

A qualified charitable organization is a nonprofit entity whose purpose is religious, charitable, educational, scientific, or literary, or which works to prevent cruelty to children or animals. Another type of qualified entity is the war veterans' organization, including posts, auxiliaries, trusts, and foundations. Yet another group of qualified organizations is domestic fraternal societies, orders, and associations operating under the lodge system, though contributions to this type of organization are only deductible if they are to be used for charitable, religious, scientific, literary, or educational purposes, or for the prevention of cruelty to children or animals. A final group of qualified entities is the United States or any state or political subdivision of a state, or Indian tribal government, though contributions are only deductible when they are to be used solely for public purposes. Examples of qualified charitable organizations are churches, United Way, nonprofit hospitals, volunteer fire companies, and museums.

EXAMPLE

Mary contributes money to her county's police force, to be used as a reward for information concerning the theft of artwork from a museum. The county police force is a qualified organization, and Mary's contribution is for a public purpose. She can deduct the contribution.

Types of Allowable Contributions

Generally, contributions can be deducted when they are made to a qualified organization, or for its use. A contribution is for the use of a qualified organization when it is held in a legally enforceable trust for the qualified organization. Out-of-pocket expenses when serving a qualified organization as a volunteer can also be deducted.

If you give property to a qualified organization, it is usually possible to deduct the fair market value of the property on the date of the contribution.

Contributions from Which You Benefit

If you receive a benefit as a result of making a contribution to a qualified organization, the allowable deduction is only that portion of the contribution that exceeds the value of the benefit received. Also, when you pay more than fair market value to a qualified organization for goods or services, the excess amount of this payment can be claimed as a deduction. For this excess amount to count as a charitable contribution, you must pay it with the intent of making a charitable contribution to the qualifying organization.

EXAMPLE

Evan pays $100 for a ticket to a social event at a local education nonprofit for disadvantaged children. The price of the ticket to just the social event is actually $30. When Evan bought the ticket, he knew that its value was less than the amount paid. The value of his charitable contribution is the difference between the $100 payment and the $30 value of the ticket, which means that he can deduct $70 as a charitable contribution to the nonprofit.

EXAMPLE

At a charity fundraiser, Margaret pays $600 for a pair of skis. The market value of the skis is the same as the price paid, so Margaret cannot claim a deductible charitable contribution.

The same principle applies to charity benefit events. If you pay an organization more than fair market value for the right to attend a charity event, such as a banquet or show, then only the excess paid over the value of the benefit received can be deducted. If there is a set price for the event, then that charge is the value of the event. If there is no set price, then its reasonable value is the value of the benefit. The amount deducted has nothing to do with whether you actually attend a charity event. A variation arises if you return the ticket to the entity for resale to someone else; in that case, the full amount paid can be deducted.

EXAMPLE

Billy pays $100 to see a special stage rendition of the classic "The Accountant in the Belfry." The ticket contains the words "Contribution - $100." If a regular ticket to the event costs $20, then the deductible amount of this ticket is $80.

You might make a contribution for which you expect to receive a state or local tax credit in return. When this is the case, you must reduce the deduction by the amount of the credit received in consideration for the payment. However, if the tax credit does not exceed 15% of the payment amount or 15% of the fair value of any transferred property, then there is no reduction of the charitable contribution.

EXAMPLE

Agnes makes a $500 contribution to a qualified organization. In exchange, she expects to receive a $300 local tax credit. This means that the amount of her deduction is reduced to $200. This reduction applies even though Agnes does not expect to claim the credit until the following year.

EXAMPLE

Xavier contributes a sculpture to a qualifying organization. On the donation date, the sculpture has a fair market value of $20,000. In return for this contribution, Xavier receives a state tax credit of $2,000, which is 10% of the fair market value of the sculpture. Since this amount does not exceed 15% of the fair market value of the sculpture, he does not have to reduce the $20,000 amount of his deduction.

The same concept applies when a donor expects to receive a state or local tax deduction (as opposed to a tax credit, as just discussed) as a result of making a contribution to a qualifying organization. If the amount of the tax deduction exceeds the amount of the contribution, then you must reduce the amount of the deduction.

It is not allowable to deduct any dues, fees, or assessments paid to a country club or similar social organization. However, it is allowable to deduct membership dues or fees paid to a qualified organization. The amount that can be deducted is only the amount paid that exceeds the value of the benefits received from the organization. However, some benefits can be disregarded if they are received in exchange for an annual payment of $75 or less, such as discounted admissions, free parking, and discounts on the purchase of goods. If the value of any benefits received relates to token items with minimal value and the qualifying organization informs you that this is the case, then the payment can be deducted in full.

Property Contributions

The general rule for property contributions is that you can deduct the fair market value of the property as of the donation date. There are several qualifications to this general rule, which are as follows:

- *Clothing and household items.* No deduction is allowed unless the items are at least in good used condition. However, a deduction is allowed when a qualified appraisal is included and the deduction is for more than $500. Household items include furniture, electronics, appliances, and linens.
- *Vehicles, boats, and airplanes.* When donating a vehicle with a fair market value over $500, the deduction is capped at the smaller of the gross proceeds from the sale of the vehicle by the organization, or the vehicle's fair market

value on the day of the contribution. There are two exceptions to these rules for deductions exceeding $500, which are as follows:

- o   You can deduct a vehicle's fair market value when the receiving organization makes a significant intervening use of it or a material improvement to it.
- o   You can deduct a vehicle's fair market value when the receiving organization gives it, or sells it for a price below fair market value, to a needy person in order to further the entity's charitable purpose.

If the organization sells the vehicle for $500 or less and the preceding exceptions do not apply, then the applicable deduction is the lesser of $500 or the vehicle's fair market value on the date of the contribution.

- *Taxidermy property*. When taxidermy property[10] is donated, the deduction is capped at the lesser of one's basis in the property or its fair market value. A taxpayer's basis in the property only includes the cost of preparing, stuffing, and mounting the property; it does not include transportation or travel costs, or the costs of hunting or killing an animal.
- *Property subject to debt*. When property is contributed that is subject to a debt (such as a mortgage), the fair value of the property must be reduced by any allowable deduction for interest that is attributable to any period following the contribution. If another party then assumes the debt, the fair value of the property must also be reduced by the outstanding amount of debt that was assumed.
- *Partial interest in a property*. Anything less than an entire interest in property cannot be deducted. Thus, the contribution of the right to use property is considered a partial interest, and so is not deductible.

EXAMPLE

Gerard owns a condominium at a golf resort and donates two weeks of its use to a qualified organization. Since Gerard still owns the building, the contribution constitutes a partial interest, which is therefore not deductible.

- *Qualified conservation contribution*. A qualified conservation contribution[11] only occurs when it is made for one of the following purposes:
  - o   The preservation of land areas for outdoor recreation by, or for the education of, the general public.

---

[10] Taxidermy property is any work of art that reproduces or preserves an animal, is prepared to recreate the characteristics of the animal, and contains a part of the body of the animal.
[11] A qualified conservation contribution is a contribution of a qualified real property interest to a qualified organization, to be used solely for conservation purposes. It must have a commitment to protect the conservation purposes of the donation and have the resources to enforce those restrictions.

- o Protecting a relatively natural habitat of fish, wildlife, or plants, or a similar ecosystem.
- o Preserving open space, if it yields a significant public benefit.
- o Preserving a historically important land area or a certified historic structure.

- *Future interest in tangible personal property*. The value of a charitable contribution of a future interest[12] in tangible personal property cannot be deducted until all intervening interests in and rights to the actual use of the property have expired or been turned over to someone other than the donor, a related person, or a related organization. Related persons include a spouse, children, grandchildren, brothers, sisters, and parents.

EXAMPLE

Samantha donates her world-famous painting collection to a museum. She gives up ownership of the paintings, but retains the right to keep the paintings in her home along with her personal sculpture collection. Since she retains an interest in the property, she cannot deduct the contribution. If Samantha later turns the paintings over to the museum, giving up all rights to their use, possession, and enjoyment, then she can take a deduction in the year in which this occurs.

- *Business inventory*. A contribution of business inventory can be deducted at the lower of its fair market value on the contribution date or its basis. The basis is any cost incurred to acquire or build the inventory. The amount of the deduction should be removed from the firm's opening inventory. The donation is not considered to be part of the firm's cost of goods sold.
- *Intellectual property*. The deduction related to a donation of intellectual property is limited to the smaller of the donor's basis in the property or its fair market value. Intellectual property includes patents, copyrights, trademarks, trade names, trade secrets, software, and similar property.

  It may be possible to claim an additional charitable contribution in later years, based on any income derived from the donated property. The percentage of income that can be deducted for each tax year ending on or after the date of the contribution appears in the following table. No additional deduction is allowed after the earlier of the 10th anniversary of the donation or the end of the property's legal life.

---

[12] A future interest is any interest that is to begin at some future date.

Deductible Percentage for Income from Donated Intangible Property

Tax Year	Deductible Percent of Income
1	100%
2	100%
3	90%
4	80%
5	70%
6	60%
7	50%
8	40%
9	30%
10	20%
11	10%
12	10%

The Determination of Fair Market Value

As just noted, a taxpayer may be able to take a deduction for contributed property that is based on its *fair market value*. This is the price at which property would be sold by a willing buyer to a willing seller, where neither party is being forced into the transaction, and where both have a reasonable knowledge of the facts pertaining to the property. Determining fair market value can be quite difficult, since there is no single formula that always applies when determining the value of property. A reasonable determination will include all facts and circumstances related to a property, such as its desirability, use, and scarcity.

EXAMPLE

Nigel wants to donate furniture for which he originally paid $5,000. The fair market value of the furniture could be quite low if it is out of style or in poor condition. Alternatively, if the furniture is now considered to be a classic and in high demand, then it is possible that a reasonable fair market value is higher than the original price at which it was acquired.

In the following bullet points, we note how fair market value is treated for different types of property:

- *Boats*. The valuation of a boat should be based on an appraisal by a marine surveyor or appraiser, since an evaluation of its physical condition is critical to its valuation.
- *Books*. The value of a book is usually derived by selecting comparable sales and adjusting the prices according to the differences between the comparable sales and the item being evaluated. This should be done by a specialized

appraiser, who will review the condition of the book, including tears, missing pages, a loose binding, stains, and so forth.

- *Cars*. The valuation of a car can be based on its "blue book" value for a private party sale. The claimed value may need to be reduced if the vehicle has engine trouble, body damage, high mileage, or any kind of excessive wear. A valuation based on a blue book value is only valid if the book lists the sale price for a car that is the same make, model, and year, sold in the same area, in the same condition, and with the same or similar options or accessories, and with similar warranties as the donated vehicle.
- *Household items*. The fair market value of household items (such as furniture and appliances) is usually quite low. Be sure to keep records to support a claimed valuation, such as cancelled checks, purchase receipts, and statements by the recipients of the items.
- *Jewelry*. Jewelry is of a highly specialized nature, so you should always obtain an appraisal from a specialized jewelry appraiser. This appraisal should describe the style, cut and setting of the jewelry, as well as whether it is now in fashion. If it is not in fashion, the appraiser should note the possibility of having the jewelry redesigned, recut or reset.
- *Paintings and objects of art*. A deduction for a painting or other object of art should be supported by an appraisal, unless the deduction is for less than $5,000. When the deduction is for $20,000 or more, the appraisal must be attached to the return. The IRS gives more weight to the opinion of an appraiser who specializes in the kind and price range of the art being appraised.
- *Patents*. The determination of fair value for a patent must take into account whether the patented technology has been rendered obsolete by other technology, whether there are any restrictions on the receiving entity's use of the technology, and the amount of time remaining before the patent expires.
- *Real estate*. Given the uniqueness of real estate, a taxpayer must obtain an appraisal from a professional appraiser. The resulting report must contain a description of the property, as well as its physical features, condition, and dimensions, how it is used, and relevant zoning. The resulting valuation can be based on comparable sales of similar properties, the capitalization of income from the property, and/or its replacement cost.
- *Used clothing*. The fair market value of used clothing is usually quite low. You should not take a deduction for clothing unless it is at least in good used condition. This value should be based on the price that the buyers of used clothes actually pay for them in used clothing stores.

A taxpayer may contribute property with a fair market value that has declined from his or her basis in it. Examples of such assets are furniture, clothing, cars, and appliances. In this case, the deduction is capped at the asset's fair market value. No deduction is allowed for the difference between the asset's basis and its fair market value.

A taxpayer may contribute property with a fair market value that has increased from his or her basis in it. When figuring the related deduction, it may be necessary to reduce the fair market value by the amount of property appreciation. The calculation depends on whether the property is classified as ordinary income property or capital gain property. The differing treatments are noted in the following bullet points:

- *Ordinary income property*. Property is classified as ordinary income property when ordinary income or a short-term capital gain would have been recognized from its sale on the date when it was contributed. Examples of ordinary income property are works of art created by the donor, inventory, and manuscripts prepared by the donor. The amount that can be deducted is a property's fair market value minus the amount that would be ordinary income or a short-term capital gain if the property were sold for its fair market value. This rule generally limits your deduction to your basis in the property.

EXAMPLE

Nora donates securities to a conservation fund that she had held for three months. The fair market value of the securities on the day of donation is $3,000, but she only paid $2,800 for them. Since the $200 of appreciation would be classified as a short-term capital gain if Nora sold the securities, her deduction is limited to $2,800; this is the fair market value of the securities, less the $200 appreciation in their value.

- *Capital gain property*. Property is classified as capital gain property if a long-term capital gain would have been recognized from its sale on the date when it was contributed. These items have typically been held for more than one year. Examples of capital gain property are securities, stamp collections, jewelry, furniture for personal use, and cars. The amount that can be deducted is the fair market value of the property. However, there are a few situations in which only the property's cost or other basis can be deducted, such as when it is intellectual property, taxidermy property, or tangible personal property that is put to an unrelated use[13] by the receiving charity.

EXAMPLE

A taxpayer contributes a sculpture to an arts training institute. If the sculpture is used by the institute to assist in the training of art students, then the sculpture is being employed for a related use. However, if the institute instead sells the sculpture and uses the proceeds for educational purposes, then it has been put to an unrelated use.

The cost or selling price of property may be a good indication of its current fair market value under the following circumstances:

- The purchase or sale took place close to the valuation date;
- The purchase or sale was at arm's length;
- Both parties knew all relevant facts;

---

[13] An unrelated use is a use unrelated to the exempt purpose of a qualified organization.

- Neither party had to engage in the transaction; and
- The relevant market did not change between the purchase or sale date and the valuation date.

The purchase or sale terms may be considered in the determination of fair market value if they had an impact on the resulting price. Examples of terms that could influence price are restrictions or covenants that limit the use or disposition of property.

It is usually assumed that the increase or decrease in the value of donated property from its original cost has been at a reasonable rate.

EXAMPLE

Emile acquired a vintage automobile for $150,000. Fifteen months later, he donates it to a car museum, claiming a charitable deduction of $200,000. The required appraisal of the automobile should include information showing that there were unusual circumstances justifying the one-third increase in value for the 15 months that Emile owned the automobile.

Fair market value can be derived from the sale of comparable properties. These sale prices are more relevant when there is a high degree of similarity between the sold and donated property. These prices are also more relevant when the time of the sale was close to the valuation date of the donated property. A further factor impacting comparability is whether the sale was at arm's length with a knowledgeable buyer and seller, where neither party was forced to take action.

EXAMPLE

George gives a first edition copy of the classic *GAAP Guidebook* to an accounting college. Being well-loved, the book is dog-eared and is missing part of its front cover. George discovers that there was a recent sale of the same book for $450. However, the book that was sold was rated in excellent condition. Although the inestimable contents of the two books are identical, their physical conditions are completely different. A knowledgeable buyer or seller would not pay much attention to the $450 sale price when evaluating the donated copy of the book.

Deduction Recapture

When all of the following statements are true, a taxpayer must recapture part of a charitable contribution deduction by adding it to his or her income:

- Tangible personal property was donated that has a claimed value of more than $5,000, and the deduction was for an amount more than one's basis in the property.
- The receiving organization then sells, trades, or otherwise disposes of the property after the year in which it was originally contributed, but within three years of the contribution.

- The receiving organization does not provide a written statement, either certifying that its use of the property was substantial and related to the entity's purpose, or certifying that its intended use of the property became impossible.

When the preceding statements are true, you should include in income the deduction claimed for the property, minus your basis in the property when the contribution was made. This amount should be included in income for the year in which the receiving organization disposed of the property.

Contributions that are Not Deductible

Several types of contributions cannot be deducted. We note these situations in the following bullet points:

- *Appraisal fees*. The cost of the fees incurred to determine the fair market value of a donated asset cannot be deducted.
- *Benefits received in exchange*. If there is an expectation of receiving a benefit from making a contribution, then that portion of the contribution comprising the value of the benefit to be received cannot be deducted. Examples of this situation are contributions to lobbying organizations or payments to a retirement home in exchange for admittance. In addition, payments made for raffle or lottery tickets are not deductible, or for any games of chance.
- *Donor-advised funds*. Donations made to a donor-advised fund are not deductible. This is a fund in which a donor can direct how donated funds are to be distributed.
- *IRA distributions*. A qualified charitable distribution from an individual retirement account (IRA) to a qualified organization is not deductible. Instead, it constitutes a non-taxable transfer out of the IRA, so that the account holder never pays income tax on the amount transferred. There is a cap on the amount of this distribution per year.
- *Nonqualified organizations*. Contributions made to non-qualified organizations are not deductible. This includes such entities as country clubs, civic leagues, chambers of commerce, political organizations, labor unions, and most foreign organizations.
- *Partial interests in property*. A contribution of less than one's entire interest in a property cannot be deducted.
- *Personal expenses*. Personal, living, or family expenses cannot be deducted. This includes the cost of meals consumed while engaged in activities for a qualified organization, unless you must be away from home on an overnight basis while engaged in volunteer activities.
- *Specific individuals*. Contributions to specific individuals are not deductible. This includes contributions made to a qualified organization for the benefit of a specific person. For example, payments made to a hospital that are directed to paying the medical bills of a specific patient are not deductible.

- *The value of your time*. A deduction for the value of your time while engaged in volunteer activities is not allowed. This includes the value of your income lost while working as an unpaid volunteer.

Penalties

A taxpayer may be liable for a penalty if the value or adjusted basis of contributed property is overstated. A 20% penalty will be applied to the amount by which your tax was underpaid due to an asset overstatement. It applies when the claimed value or adjusted basis amount is 150% or more of the correct amount, and the related tax underpayment was more than $5,000.

A 40% penalty will instead be applied when the claimed value or adjusted basis amount is 200% or more of the correct amount, and the related tax underpayment was more than $5,000.

> **Note:** An appraiser who prepares an incorrect appraisal may have to pay a penalty if the person should have known that the appraisal would be used to claim a refund, and the appraisal results in the 20% or 40% penalties for valuation misstatement.

Substantiation Requirements

Records must be maintained to provide evidence of the amount of contributions made during the year. The types of records kept depends on the amounts donated and whether they were cash contributions, noncash contributions, or out-of-pocket expenses when donating your personal services. In the following sub-sections, we note the substantiation requirements for each of these types of donations.

> **Note:** As a general rule, the receiving entity must provide a written statement when it receives a payment of more than $75 that is partly a contribution and partly for goods or services.

Substantiation of Cash Contributions

A cash contribution cannot be deducted unless at least one of the following is retained as a form of substantiation:

- *Bank record*. A bank record that shows the name of the receiving entity, the date of the contribution, and the amount paid. This can take the form of a cancelled check, bank statement, or credit card statement.
- *Receipt*. A receipt from the receiving entity, stating the name of the organization, the date of the contribution, and the amount paid.
- *Payroll deduction*. When a contribution is made by payroll deduction, retain a pay stub or Form W-2 that shows the date and amount of the contribution, as well as a pledge card that shows the name of the receiving entity and which states that it does not provide goods or services in exchange for any contributions made.

When a contribution is made for $250 or more, a contemporaneous written acknowledgement of the contribution from the receiving party is required. Do not combine separate contributions when determining whether at least $250 has been paid. When contributions are made by payroll deduction, the deduction linked to each paycheck is considered a separate contribution.

EXAMPLE

Jonathan donates $30 per week to a local charity. Each payment is considered a separate contribution, so he does not reach the $250 threshold.

A written acknowledgement must include the amount of the contribution, whether the receiving entity gave the taxpayer any goods or services resulting from the contribution, and a description and estimate of the value of any goods and services provided to the taxpayer by the entity. In order for an acknowledgement to be considered contemporaneous, it must be received on or before the earlier of the date when the taxpayer files his or her return for the year in which the contribution was made, or the due date (including extensions) for filing the return.

Substantiation of Noncash Contributions

When a noncash contribution is made, the amount of required substantiation depends on the size of the related deduction. The requirements are as follows:

- *Less than $250*. Obtain a receipt that shows the name and address of the receiving entity, the date and location of the contribution, and a description of the property. For a security, also note the name of the issuer, the type of security, and whether it is publicly traded.
- *$250 to $500*. Obtain a written acknowledgement that includes a description of the property, whether any goods or services were given in exchange, and a description and estimate of the value of any goods or services provided.
- *$500+ to $5,000*. Complete Form 8283, *Noncash Charitable Contributions*, and obtain the written acknowledgement just described.
- *$5,000+*. Complete Form 8283, *Noncash Charitable Contributions*, obtain the written acknowledgement just described, and a qualified written appraisal of the property from a qualified appraiser[14].

Substantiation of Out-of-Pocket Expenses

When a taxpayer incurs out-of-pocket expenses as part of providing services to a qualified organization, and the amount is for $250 or more, then the person must have adequate records to prove the amount of the expenses. In addition, the receiving

---

[14] A qualified appraiser is someone with verifiable education and experience in valuing the type of property for which an appraisal is performed.

organization must issue an acknowledgement that contains a description of the services provided, and a statement of whether or not it provided any goods or services in exchange (and their value).

If car expenses are being claimed, then a taxpayer must keep reliable written records of the expenses incurred. To be reliable, the records should have been made regularly and at or near the time when the expenses were incurred. This may involve the name of the organization being served, the dates of car usage, and the miles driven. Or, if actual expenses are being deducted, then the records should include those costs of operating the car that relate directly to the indicated charitable purpose.

Summary

A taxpayer may benefit greatly from making deductions associated with a variety of charitable contributions. To ensure that these deductions are acceptable, you must ensure that contributions are made to qualified charitable organizations, donated property is correctly valued, and supporting documentation is retained. In addition, donations are capped at a percentage of your adjusted taxable income – which varies depending on the circumstances. In short, a detailed knowledge of the information noted in this chapter is needed in order to maximize your deductions from charitable contributions.

Glossary

A

Annuity. A financial product that pays out a fixed stream of payments to an individual. It is primarily used as an income stream for retirees.

Asset class. A grouping of investments that exhibit similar characteristics and are subject to the same laws and regulations.

B

Back-end load. A fee paid when selling mutual fund shares.

Bear market. A condition when asset prices fall by at least 20% over a period of at least two months.

Bond. A fixed obligation to pay that is issued by a corporation or government entity to investors.

Bull market. A condition when asset prices rise at least 20% over a sustained period of time.

C

Call option. A contract that gives you the right, but not the obligation, to buy stock at a predetermined price within a specific range of dates.

Cash surrender value. The amount of money that a life insurance company pays out to a policy holder if they decide to end the plan.

Certificate of deposit. A term bank deposit with a fixed duration and a stated interest rate.

Charitable contribution. A donation or gift to, or for the use of, a qualified organization.

Collectibles. Items worth more than they were originally sold for, due to their rarity or popularity.

D

Depreciation. The planned, gradual reduction in the recorded value of an asset over its useful life by charging it to expense.

Dividend. A payment to shareholders of a portion of a corporation's earnings.

Dollar-cost averaging. An investment strategy in which an investor consistently invests a fixed amount of money into a particular asset at regular intervals, regardless of its price, aiming to reduce the impact of market volatility over time.

Glossary

E

Economic indicator. Economic data used to interpret the current or future state of the economy.

Efficient market hypothesis. A theory that the markets always incorporate all information, so it is impossible to beat the market.

Emerging markets. Rapidly-developing countries with young populations and increasing living standards.

Exchange-traded fund. A mutual fund that invests in a particular index, industry, or commodity.

F

Fair market value. The price at which property would be sold by a willing buyer to a willing seller, where neither party is being forced into the transaction, and where both have a reasonable knowledge of the facts pertaining to the property.

First-to-die policy. When several people are insured under one policy, with the insurer paying out when the first person dies.

Four percent rule. A rule which states that retirees can safely withdraw an amount equal to four percent of their savings in each year.

Future interest. Any interest that is to begin at some future date.

H

Hedge fund. An entity that pools the money of contributing investors and tries to achieve above-market returns through a wide variety of investment strategies.

I

Investment risk. The probability of occurrence of losses relative to the expected return on an investment.

M

Money market fund. A type of mutual fund that restricts its investments to highly liquid, near-term instruments.

Mutual fund. A type of financial vehicle that is made up of a pool of money obtained from a large number of investors; its goal is to invest the money in a variety of securities.

P

Penny stock. A small company's stock that trades for less than $5 per share, and which trades over-the-counter.

Personal property. Property that is movable, and so may include furniture and fixtures, vehicles, and collectibles.

Glossary

Portfolio rebalancing. The process of returning the values of a portfolio's asset allocations to the levels defined by an investment plan.

Put option. A contract that gives its holder the right, but not the obligation, to sell stock at a strike price, before the option's expiration date.

R

Real estate investment trust. A company that owns, operates, or finances income-generating property.

Real property. Any property that is directly attached to the land, plus land itself.

S

Sales load. The commission charged to an investor when buying shares in a mutual fund.

SEC yield. A standard yield calculation used for the fair comparison of bonds.

Sector rotation. An investment strategy that involves shifting portfolio allocations among different industry sectors based on the expected performance of each sector during various phases of the economic cycle.

Share. A unit of stock.

Short sale. When a homeowner sells his or her property to a third party for less than the amount due on the associated mortgage, with all proceeds going to the lender.

Speculation. When you make an investment that has a significant risk of loss, but for which there is also an expectation of a significant gain.

Speculative bubble. A spike in asset values that is fueled by irrational speculative activity that is not supported by the fundamentals.

Stock. A security that represents the ownership of a fraction of a corporation.

Stock index. A group of shares that are used to give an indication of the stock market as a whole or a subset of it.

Stock market. The collection of exchanges at which the shares of publicly-traded companies are bought and sold.

T

Tax-loss harvesting. The sale of securities at a loss in order to offset the amount of capital gains tax owed from the sale of profitable assets.

Timeshare. A form of fractional ownership, where buyers purchase the right to occupy a unit of real estate over specified periods.

V

Venture capital fund. A corporate entity that pools the cash contributions of multiple investors and institutions for investments in startup companies.

Y

Yield curve. A graphical representation of the yields on a bond, based on its maturity date.

Put options 81

Qualified charitable distributions 97
Qualified charitable organizations 109

Raw land 85
Real estate investment
      Advantages 62
      Disadvantages 64
Real estate investment trust 77
Real property 102
Required minimum distributions 97
Residence, conversion to rental 66
Residence, purchase of 66
Residential property, flipping 70
Residential property, purchase of 69
Retirement 4
Risk issues 28
Risk profile 5
Roll up strategy 38
Roth IRA 88

Savings accounts 43
Second home, purchase of 67
Sector rotation 15
SEP IRA 91
Short sale 75
SIMPLE IRA 91
Socially responsible investing 99

Speculation 23
Speculative bubbles 40
Stock fund fundamentals 58
Stock market 34
Stock options 39
Stock purchase plan 39
Substantiation requirements 119

Tax-loss harvesting 14
Technical analysis strategy 38
Thematic investments 100
Theme investment strategy 38
Timberland investments 85
Timeshare, purchase of 68
Timing of goals 3
Treasury bills 50
Treasury notes 50
Types of allowable contributions 109

Undeveloped land, purchase of 71
Upgrade and sell your home 67

Value strategy 37
Venture capital 83

Withdrawal plans 4
Works of art 84

Yield curve 48

Index

Ability to contribute 92
Advisor evaluation............................... 20
Advisory fees...................................... 19
Allowable distributions 96
Annuity... 107

Bear market 36
Bond features...................................... 46
Bond fund fundamentals....................... 59
Bond fund selection process 60
Bonds, types of.................................. 45
Bull market.. 36

Call options.. 81
Cash flow projection............................ 12
Certificates of deposit........................... 44
Certified Financial Planner 18
Characteristics of stocks 34
Collectibles.. 84
Commercial property, purchase of 70
Contribution caps 93
Contribution deductibility 94
Contributions not deducted................. 118
Contributions with benefits 110
Currency investments 81

Debt reduction 28
Deduction recapture............................ 117
Dollar-cost averaging 15

Early distribution penalties................... 96
Equity risk 25
Excess contributions............................ 94
Exchange-traded fund........................... 40

Fair market value............................... 114
FDIC insurance................................... 30
Financial advisors............................... 17
Financial policies................................. 2
Fixed income risk 24
Foreclosure.. 72
Funding tranches 3

Growth strategy 37

Hedge funds 82
How businesses add value....................32
How businesses raise money.................32
How to buy bonds 51
Hybrid funds 61

Income strategy..................................37
Individual retirement account 87
Installment sale 76
Interest taxability................................97
Investing performance..........................42
Investing strategies.............................37
Investment best practices 55
Investment management style 8
Investment principles 22
Investment risk...................................24
Investment strategy 13
Investment types 26

Lending arrangements..........................27
Leverage..14
Life insurance
    Types of...106
    When to use....................................105
Life planning.......................................1
Lifestyle costs 4
Liquidity analysis................................10

Market moving events..........................35
Merger arbitrage strategy 38
Money manager performance 41
Money market fund..............................44
Mutual funds......................................40
Mutual funds vs. ETFs.........................53

Penalties 119
Penny stocks.......................................41
Personal property 102
Plan adjustments 13
Planning assumptions...........................11
Portfolio rebalancing............................13
Precious metals 83
Probate sale.......................................74
Property contributions.........................111
Property insurance..............................102